I0813983

HITLER'S HEADQUARTERS IN THE WEST

THEN AND NOW

HITLER'S HEADQUARTERS IN THE WEST

THEN AND NOW

by Jean Paul Pallud

An Imprint of Pen & Sword Books Ltd

Hitler's Headquarters in the West – Then and Now

Published by After the Battle
An imprint of Pen & Sword Books Ltd
Yorkshire – Philadelphia
Website: **www.afterthebattle.com**
www.pen-and-sword.co.uk

ISBN: 978-1-03610-133-6

Commissioning Editor: Rob Green
Editor: Jean Paul Pallud
Design: Paul Wilkinson
Cover design: Jon Wilkinson

Credits:
Parts of this book were originally published as articles in *After the Battle* magazine: 'Obersalzberg' edited by Winston Ramsey in issue 9 (August 1975), 'The Führerhautpquartiere' by Richard Raiber in issue 19 (November 1977), 'The Führerhautpquartier Wolfsschlucht 2' in issue 149 (August 2010) and 'The Führerhautpquartier Wolfsschlucht 3' in issue 180 (May 2018). These have been adapted and enhanced to produce this book and 150 additional photos are included.

Acknowledgements:
The Editor would like to acknowledge Internet contributors, and more particularly Wikimedia Commons contributors, for the remarkable photos they make available to all. The Editor extends his appreciation to Didier Ledé of the ASW2 Association, Marc Doucet, Jean-Paul Brillard, Jean-Pierre Gort, the Brûly-de-Pesche 1940 Association, Pierre Rhode and Werner Sünkel, authors of *Wolfsschlucht 2, Autopsie eines Führerhauptquartiers*, and Dieter Zeigert and Franz Seidler, authors of *Die Führerhauptquartiere 1939-1945*.

Photo Credit Abbreviations:
BA – Bundesarchiv; ECPAD – Médiathèque de la Défense, Fort d'Ivry; SETO – Society for the Study of the ETO; USNA – US National Archives. Parts of these photos, credited as ATB/USNA, are from negatives obtained in the 1970s by ATB from the collection of seized enemy documents. Unless specified otherwise, all illustrations are from the *After the Battle* archive.

Front Cover: 'Wolfsschlucht 2' , Führerhauptquartier for one day. On June 17, 1944, Hitler came in person to FHQu 'W 2' to meet with Generalfeldmarschall von Rundstedt, commander-in-Chief West, and Generalfeldmarschall Rommel, the commander of Heeresgruppe B. The meeting took place in this bunker at 9.30 a.m. and lasted till 12.30 p.m. when lunch was served in the nearby Teehaus. The talks resumed in the afternoon but were soon interrupted by an air raid warning. Unfortunately, no photographs appear to have been taken that day but a team from the US 602nd Engineer Camouflage Battalion took this nice picture of Bau 1 in September 1944, a few days after the last Germans had left. (USNA)

Back Cover:
Top: Hitler and his FHQu staff moved to 'Wolfsschlucht' at Brûly-de-Pesche on June 6, 1940. This name is misleading for today's readers as Hitler used two FHQu named 'Wolfsschlucht': 'Wolfsschlucht' at Brûly-de-Pesche in June 1940, and he went one day to 'Wolfsschlucht 2' at Margival in June 1944. Hitler and Engel stretch their legs in front of the Brûly-de-Pesche church (just off to the left in this photo).

Bottom: Another photo taken by the US investigation team at 'Wolfsschlucht 2', of a bunker camouflaged to merge in with the hillside behind. The Teehaus appears in the top left corner. Without the Teehaus, it would have been difficult to identify this particular bunker for they were all built along the same general lines. It is in fact the western end of Bau 5, the huge bunker housing the complex's telephone exchange.

CONTENTS

Hitler and his inner circle at FHQu 'Felsennest' where he resided from May 10 to June 5. Visible in the right part of the photo, the door giving access to the Lagebaracke through the inclined camouflage cover identifies this photo as undoubtedly being taken at FHQu 'Felsennest'.

INTRODUCTION

THE FÜHRERHAUPTQUARTIERE, the Führer's Headquarters, officially abbreviated FHQu, were the various command posts from which Adolf Hitler directed the German war effort. In 1939, he played very little part in the direction of military operations in the campaign in Poland but this changed at the beginning of 1940 and from 1941, military command rested upon his directives.

The nature and size of the FHQu followed Hitler's implication in the direction of military operations, ranging from the simple Führersonderzug, the Führer's special train, of 1939 to the vast concrete complex 'Wolfsschanze' in East Prussia where he stayed for most of 1942, 1943 and 1944.

According to a secret report written in November 1944 by Hauptbauleiter Siegfried Schmelcher, Chefbaumeister der Führerhauptquartieranlagen (Senior Construction Engineer of the Führerhauptquartier Projects), the Organisation Todt built a total of 16 Führerhauptquartiere throughout the territory of the Reich and the occupied areas, and three more were still in construction in early 1945.

In order not to be limited by the size of a single book, we decided to divide the subject into two. Here is the history of the Führerhauptquartiere in the West, and another book will tell the story of the FHQu in the East. The partition is somewhat artificial, with West and East defined by a straight line drawn on a map, but it also had a reality: the Third Reich fought a war on two fronts, the West, and the East.

The Schmelcher's report provides a rich historical perspective of the construction work of the FHQu and to explain this, we have woven the clear and rigid approach of this report with the story of Hitler and his entourage staying, or not, in the successive FHQu. In some cases, dozens of photos were taken, at 'Felsennest' or 'Wolfsschlucht' for example, sometimes few or no photographs were taken.

We will see in this book how Hitler, secluded in his austere FHQu, gradually lost touch with reality, eventually directing attacks with forces that did not exist. We will see him coming to FHQu 'Wolfsschlucht 2' in June 1944, to meet Generalfeldmarschall von Rundstedt and Rommel, the commanders in the West, and remained deaf to their warnings, simply finding fault with the local commanders in the failure to counter the Allied landings.

In December 1944, we will see Albert Speer describing how Hitler was 'in the grip of a permanent euphoria' at FHQu 'Adlerhorst', repeating optimistic forecasts for 1945 and 'his followers, including myself' wrote Speer, 'were transported in spite of all their scepticism into a more sanguine state'. We will see Generaloberst Heinz Guderian, then head of the Generalstabes des

Hitler resided at FHQu 'Wolfsschlucht' from June 6 to June 25. Brûly-de-Pesche, near the Saint-Méen fountain: Generaloberst Keitel, Chief of OKW, Hitler, Generalmajor Jodl, Chief of the Operations Staff of the OKW, and Major Engel, OKH Adjutant, study a report.

Heeres, coming twice to FHQu 'Adlerhorst' in January 1945 to warn Hitler of the threat of a Soviet breakthrough in northwest Hungary. He insisted that forces be transferred to the East before it was too late, but Hitler refused.

A warning to end this introduction. These photos of banal discussions and walks in the reclusive and well-regulated world of the FHQu should not make us forget that the men we see were the masters of the Nazi regime and the managers of its horrors, its concentration camps, its mass shootings of Jews in the East, its extermination camps.

Jean Paul Pallud

THE BERGHOF, BERCHTESGADEN

SWORN IN AS REICHSKANZLER (Chancellor) in 1933, upon Hidenburg's death on August 2, 1934, Hitler became Reichskanzler and Reichspräsident (Reich President) in temporary personal union. He then abolished the title of Reichspräsident in favour of Führer, a title without precedent in German history, and he then had the two offices of Reichskanzler and Führer fused. The changes – none of them constitutionally legitimate – were legitimised by means of a plebiscite on August 19.

The Reichswehr was reorganised as the Wehrmacht in May 1935, bringing the army, navy, and air force under unified command. In January 1938 the Defence Minister, General Werner von Blomberg, was forced to resign his posts (Hitler was presented with evidence that von Blomberg's new wife had posed in the past for pornographic photos). On February 4 Hitler signed a decree that announced: 'Henceforth I exercise power of command over the Wehrmacht personally. The former Wehrmacht Office in the Reich War Ministry, together with its duties, becomes the Wehrmacht High Command and is my military Staff immediately under my command.' On this day, Hitler united political and military power in his own person.

A newly created Higher General Staff, the Oberkommando der Wehrmacht, OKW (Supreme Command of the Armed Forces) was interposed between Hitler and the OKH (Army High Command), OKM (High Command of the Navy), and OKL (High Command of the Air Force). The functions of OKW were to correlate and supervise the individual strategies as conceived and initiated by the three services. The most important department of the OKW was the Wehrmachtführungsamt, WFA, later Wehrmachtführungsstab, WFSt (Armed Forces Operations Office, later Staff).

In 1939, for the campaign in Poland, Hitler played very little part in the direction of military operations but this changed at the beginning of 1940. Thenceforth, he listened to the reports at the daily situation conferences which had generally been prepared by the Wehrmachtführungsstab, elicited, and weighed the responses of the service professionals who participated in the discussions which followed. He then announced his decisions. OKW became little more than a secretariat which translated these decisions into Orders or Directives which the General Staffs of the services were then obliged to process for execution.

The Führerhauptquartiere, officially abbreviated FHQu (Führer's Headquarters), were the various command posts from which Hitler directed

In February 1938, a decree announced that Hitler 'personally exercises the power of command over the Wehrmacht'. From then on, he united political and military power in his own person. A propaganda postcard, 'Der Führer im Kampfgelände', the Führer on the battlefield.

the war effort. The FHQu was Hitler, the OKW, the service liaison officers to the Führer, and his service and personal adjutants. OKH, OKM, and OKL were the invited guests to the Führerhauptquartier, and often they were physically located many kilometres distant.

It is interesting to note how, from 1941, the Führerhauptquartier was far from the Oberste Heeresleitung, OHL (General Headquarters), the highest German military command centre in the First World War. In 1914, Kaiser Wilhelm II was nominally the Oberster Kriegsherr (Supreme War Lord) but he was expected to act in that capacity in accordance with the professional advice of the Chef des Generalstabes des Feldheeres (Chief of the General Staff of the Field Army), the German Army's highest general. In practice the Kaiser interfered very little, initially, and later not at all, in the military sphere. Thus, in 1914-1918, OHL was the Army General Staff over which its Chef presided, and the Kaiser was scarcely more than its invited guest.

By 1941, Hitler was Oberster Kriegsherr to an extent to which Wilhelm II could never have aspired.

We have chosen to retain the historical German abbreviated name, FHQu, but this raises the question of which plural to use. It should be FHQu's in English, which is not really smooth. We therefore decided to use FHQu also in the plural, knowing that the sentence will allow you to understand whether it refers to one FHQu, or to several. However, for the few times we use the full name, Führerhauptquartier, we chose to use the German plural, Führerhauptquartiere, when we refer to several of them.

Hitler spent very little time in Berlin after the war began, especially after June 1941, and was most frequently at the Berghof in Berchtesgaden or at the 'Wolfschanze' headquarters in East Prussia.

Hitler's connection with the Obersalzberg, a quiet mountain retreat above Berchtesgaden, began after his unsuccessful attempt to seize power in

The small cabin called the 'Kampfhaus' on Obersalzberg where Hitler wrote his book *Mein Kampf* after his release from Landsberg prison. No trace of it is left today.

Munich in November 1923. He was subsequently imprisoned at Landsberg, and after his release in 1925, he sought refuge in the Obersalzberg. He then stayed in a small cottage called the Kampfhaus and wrote the second part of *Mein Kampf* there.

In 1928, he was living in another house, Haus Wachenfeld, which he initially rented, but the royalties from his book allowed him to buy it in 1933. He then began to rebuild the chalet which would become known as the Berghof (Mountain Court). After coming to power in January 1933, he commissioned Rudolf Hess, his secretary, to negotiate with local farmers the purchase of their property on the Obersalzberg. Those unwilling to

Royalties from his book allowed Hitler to buy Haus Wachenfeld in 1933. The house, which became the Berghof, was given another floor and wide steps were built leading up to the front of the building.

Sworn in as chancellor in 1933, Hitler became Reichspräsident upon the death of Hindenburg in 1934, and he then abolished the latter title in favour of the Führer. Propaganda photograph of the Führer receiving members of a Hitler Youth orchestra at the Berghof.

In the early years, crowds of admirers were allowed on the road leading to the Berghof and Hitler greeted them from the Berghof. In June 1937 Bormann had a mature linden tree planted near the end of the driveway to provide some shade on the hot summer days (tree not seen in this picture).

sell soon did so under pressure and threats from the Nazi Party. Within a short time, ten square kilometres were acquired from private owners, the forest administration, and the municipality of Salzberg.

When Hess was assigned to other tasks, Martin Bormann took over the Obersalzberg project. Country houses and mountain farms were replaced with administrative buildings and barracks for SS guards, a hotel was rebuilt to accommodate visiting dignitaries, and housing was built for the many workers. The steep road leading from Berchtesgaden to Obersalzberg was widened and a new road was built to Oberau. Hitler insisted that any construction should not affect the natural balance of the area.

In a series of extensions and renovations, the once modest Berghof was given another floor and wide steps were built leading up to the front of the building. A room with heavy marble pillars formed the lobby of a large

Furnished with Persian rugs and paintings, the main hall served as a reception and conference room. This view shows the southwest corner of the room, with the open fireplace on the south wall (left) and the door to original part of the building, Haus Wachenfeld, on the west wall (right). The painting Venus and Love by Paris Bordone, which appeared to the right of the fireplace in this photograph, was bought by Hitler in 1936. At the end of the war, this painting was given to Poland and it can be seen today at the National Museum in Warsaw. On the west wall, to the right of the door, was a large Gobelins tapestry – Gobelin is a famous French tapestry maker – whose historical and mythical scenes Hitler appreciated. It seems that the fate of this tapestry is not known, destroyed in the last days of the war or taken by someone and now part of a private collection or museum? It is, however, possible that this tapestry was not a real Gobelin, but a fake.

conference room, where a giant window could be lowered to provide a panoramic view of the mountains. In addition, the ground floor contained the vestibule, the dining room, the guard room, a day room for the staff, a large kitchen, two rooms for adjutants, and an outdoor terrace. Hitler's living room, bedroom, study, and rooms for his permanent bodyguard occupied the first floor, with the second floor reserved for more personal guests. Reconstructions and modifications to the Berghof continued even during the war, when building materials were scarce.

Many Nazi leaders had also purchased properties on the Obersalzberg. Göring had a house built in 1934, and Bormann moved in 1937 with his family into a villa that the Party had just purchased. Speer occupied another villa which the Party acquired in 1937. The Party also acquired the Gasthaus zum Türken which, after renovation work in 1937, fulfilled the dual function of a communications centre and quarters for security units.

Göring often stayed at his residence in Obersalzberg, even if only for a

Facing north, a large bay window offered a magnificent view of the mountains and valleys. It could be lowered to allow an uninterrupted view.

few days between official functions. His visits would not be heralded by the closure of roads, as were Hitler's, and he would arrive accompanied only by his driver, or a small escort. His wife, Emmy Göring, stayed several months at a time at the Obersalzberg residence, but she did not mix with either the Bormann family or Eva Braun, whom she openly despised.

The 'Führer area', surrounded by a two-metre-high fence, was divided into two parts. The inner area, which contained the Berghof and Bormann's house, was guarded by SS sentries. The outer perimeter was initially guarded by civilian police, later replaced by the Reichssicherheitsdienst, the State Security Service. Passes had to be shown upon entry to the Führer area, and one of Bormann's instructions was that 'a uniform is not permission to pass these gates'.

With the Obersalzberg complex assuming a major importance in the government of the Third Reich, a Reichskanzlei (Reich Chancellery) was built in 1936-37 at Stanggass, just north-west of Berchtesgaden, to serve as a diplomatic centre. It was surrounded by a small complex of staff and security buildings. This complex included houses for Generaloberst Wilhelm Keitel (Generalfeldmarschall from July 1940), Chief of the Oberkommando der Wehrmacht (OKW), and Generalmajor Alfred Jodl (General der Artillerie from July 1940, Generaloberst in 1944), Chief of the Operations Staff of the OKW.

Tea time on the Berghof terrace with friends, summer 1938. On the left, Bormann. (ATB/USNA)

The Berghof terrace, summer of 1940, from left to right: Albert Speer, Theodor Morell, Hitler, and Hermann Esser. Speer was then head of the Chief Office for Construction (he was appointed Minister of Armaments and War Production in February 1942). Morell was Hitler's personal physician and Esser was State Secretary for Tourism in Goebbels' Propaganda Ministry.

Another of the projects realised on the Obersalzberg under Bormann's direction was the construction of dwellings for personnel. The Klaushöhe settlement was begun in 1941 and the Buchenhöhe settlement in 1942.

Building the Kehlsteinhaus on the top of the Kehlstein Mountain was Bormann's idea. A road six kilometres long was carved out of virgin rock

Bormann was behind the idea of building a teahouse on the 1,834-metre high Kehlstein mountain. To get from the parking area to the mountain peak above, a marble-clad tunnel was driven 126 metres into the rock leading to a lobby from where a lift transported visitors 124 metres up to the interior of the teahouse. Received there in 1938, French Ambassador André François-Poncet coined the name 'Eagle's Nest' for the building.

Blasted out of solid rock between 1937 and 1938, with five tunnels along the way, the road was an amazing feat of engineering. This photo was taken on September 16, 1938, from a convoy car climbing the winding road to the parking lot at the foot of the summit. Hitler, on his way to inaugurate the Kehlsteinhaus, was in the car out front.

Hitler chatting with intimates in the main reception room and relaxing on the south-facing sun terrace. (ATB/USNA)

and snaked through several tunnels and hairpin bends to a parking lot below the summit of the mountain. From there, a tunnel dug into the rock led to an elevator which took the visitors 124 metres higher, directly to the reception of the building. The Kehlsteinhaus consisted of a dining room, an office, a living room, a kitchen, a guard room, a rest room, washrooms and a large basement. There was an independent generator and a hot air heating system.

Hitler visited the newly built Kehlsteinhaus for thc first timc on September 16, 1938. In October, he received the French Ambassador André François-Poncet there and it was he who coined the name 'Eagle's Nest' for the building. Hitler returned rarely to the Kehlsteinhaus – sources say he made only 14 visits, and most of them in the first year – but Bormann often spent his Sundays there and received some foreign

This photo was taken either in the wood-paneled dining room which had four windows opening onto the sun terrace, or in Hitler's study which had two. (ATB/USNA)

Hitler shows the newly completed Kehlsteinhau to Robert Ley, head of the Deutsche Arbeitsfront (German Labour Front) and Gauleiter Alfred Wagner. One of the Old Figthers (Alten Kämpfer), and part of the circle of intimates invited to the Berghof, Gauleiter Wagner was Reich Defence Commissioner for Military Districts VII and XIII. Left was Frau Ley and daughter, and right Bormann (partly visible) and SS-Gruppenführer Julius Schaub, Hitler's personal Adjutant. (Florian Beierl)

If Hitler seldom used the Kehlsteinhaus, Bormann often went up there. Here, he is seen on the terrace. Seated on the left was Goebbels in conversation with his private secretary, Werner Naumann. (Florian Beierl)

visitors. Eva Braun also attended the Eagle's Nest and a wedding party was held there after the marriage of her sister Gretl to Hermann Fegelein in June 1944.

Hitler received diplomats or foreign statesmen at the Berghof, such as British Prime Minister Neville Chamberlain on September 15, 1938, who, to appease him, gave verbal agreement to the annexation of the Sudetenland by the Reich.

On September 20, Hitler received Béla Imrédy, Hungarian Prime Minister, and, later in the afternoon, Józef Lipski, Polish Ambassador to Germany. The press release regarding the reception of the Hungarian Prime Minister included most of the issues raised, but only the fact that the Polish ambassador had been received was mentioned in the second press release.

On November 24, 1938, Hitler received King Carol II of Romania and, on June 17, 1939, Khalid Al Hud, special envoy of King Ibn Saud of Saudi Arabia.

Hitler was at the Berghof in August 1939 when Reich Foreign Minister Joachim von Ribbentrop negotiated the German-Soviet pact with Soviet Foreign Minister Vyacheslav Molotov in Moscow.

The long and wide staircase leading from the driveway to the Berghof entrance was the scene of many famous photos, here a posed photo with the Duke and Duchess of Windsor on October 22, 1937. Just to Hitler's left, in a white raincoat, was Robert Ley, the head of the German Labour Front, who had invited the Duke and Duchess to tour Germany and who served as their host and personal chaperone.

In August 1938, Hitler received Marshal Italo Balbo, Governor-General of Italian Libya and Commander-in-Chief of Italian North Africa, at the Berghof. Balbo was among a minority of leading Fascists to oppose Mussolini's alliance with Nazi Germany. (ATB/USNA)

Balbo, Eugen Dollmann, interpreter, here with the rank of SS-Obersturmführer, and Hitler. ATB/USNA)

More historical photos on the staircase leading from the driveway to the Berghof, here British Prime Minister Neville Chamberlain on September 15, 1938. During the following conference, Chamberlain verbally gave Hitler his agreement on the annexation of the Sudetenland by the Third Reich.

The visitors' car parked on the driveway, just in front of the staircase. Bormann (right) welcomed Italian officials in great uniform in 1938. (ATB/USNA)

On July 18, 1940, Hitler went down to his car which was waiting for him at this same location before his departure for Berlin. The tall man standing in the car with a movie camera was Walter Frentz. Having worked as a cameraman on the famous film Olympia about the 1936 Berlin Olympics, from 1939 Frentz was closely associated with photographing and filming the Third Reich personalities.

With Hitler the supreme commander, the Berghof was the de facto Führerhauptquartier on the frequent occasions when Hitler was staying there. Situation conference on July 29, 1940: General der Artillerie Alfred Jodl, Chief of the Operations Staff of the OKW; General der Artillerie Franz Halder, Chief-of-Staff of OKH; Hitler; Generalfeldmarschall Wilhelm Keitel, Chief of OKW; Generalfeldmarschall Walther von Brauchitsch, Chief of OKH.

On May 11, 1941, Hitler received at the Berghof Admiral François Darlan, number 2 in the regime of Maréchal Philippe Pétain, French head of state. Later in May, he received Edoardo Alfieri, Italian Ambassador to Germany and other Italian diplomats for the second anniversary of the Pact of Steel. In June, he met with Croatian head of state Ante Pavelic.

THE INVASION OF POLAND, 1939, FÜHRERSONDERZUG

HITLER RECEIVED HIS FIRST Staats-Sonderzug (State Special Train) in 1933 or 1934. Progressively, every minister or department became entitled to having his own special train – Göring, von Ribbentrop, Himmler, the OKW and OKH, and many more – and a comprehensive building programme of 'Sonderzüge' was undertaken. In 1941 they were 25 Sonderzüge, with a total approaching 400 cars.

Oberstleutnant Nicolaus von Vormann, liaison officer at the Führer Headquarters during the Polish campaign, detailed the composition of the Führersonderzug: 'I never went into the leading coach, which was occupied by Hitler and his personal staff. The second wagon was the operations coach, with the forward half a room with a large map table, three telephones and some movable easy chairs. The telephone exchange and signals centre occupied the rear half. Next came the sleeping car for the SS bodyguard, two more sleeping cars for adjutants, doctors, soldiers and so on, and a dining car. The rest of the train was taken over by Reich Press Chief Otto Dietrich. At each end were special wagons with light flak guns under an armoured canopy.' On September 12, 1939, the Führersonderzug was parked on a siding at Illnau, Silesia, and von Ribbentrop and Hitler conferred in the fresh air in company with Walther Hewel, the Foreign Minister's envoy to the Führerhauptquartier.

Göring visited the Führer Headquarters on September 13. On the right, Walter Frentz and his camera. He served as a Luftwaffe cameraman throughout the war, and in 1939 and 1940 he was tasked with filming Hitler and his FHQu.
(ATB/USNA)

No documents describing the exact components of the Führersonderzug in September 1939 are available, but the elements of 'Bln 2009' (which departed Anhalter Bahnhof in Berlin at 12.30 p.m. on June 23, 1941 and arrived at Rastenburg, East Prussia at 1.30 a.m. June 24) are known: behind two locomotives in tandem came a special Flakwagen, each end of which had an open platform on which an anti-aircraft gun was in position.

Next came a baggage car, followed by the Führerwagen for Hitler's personal use (with the main room at the baggage car end), then a Befehlswagen (command car). This included a conference room with map tables and a compartment for the communications centre. Next came a Begleitkommandowagen for the Führer-Begleit-Kommando, the bodyguard unit tasked with guarding Hitler and his field headquarters, a dining car, two cars for guests, a Badewagen (bathing car), another dining car, two sleeping cars for enlisted personnel, a Pressewagen (car for the press), another baggage car, and finally a second Flakwagen. When the Führersonderzug passed through a station in which the direction of travel was changed, the cars then travelled in the reverse order.

The Führersonderzug left Berlin at 9.00 p.m. on September 3, 1939, three days after the attack on Poland had begun. Hitler, some of his close

In the operations coach, Hitler looks on when Generaloberst Keitel presents Göring with the situation at the front and the developments. (ATB/USNA)

collaborators, the OKW leadership, the Führer's adjutants, and a close security team, the Kriminalkommando, were on board.

Generals Keitel and Jodl of the OKW were quartered aboard the train but the OKH was only represented on board by Hauptmann Gerhard Engel, the Führer's Heeresadjutant. Thus, the two main OKH generals at that time, Generaloberst Walther von Brauchitsch (Oberbefehlshaber des Heeres), and General der Artillerie Franz Halder (Chef des Generalstabes des Heeres),

On the 15th, Hitler flew to the San River and at Ubieszyn, 20 kilometres north of Jaroslaw, he climbed onto a small mound to observe troops crossing the river. (ATB/USNA)

On the 13th, in the company of General Johannes Blaskowitz, commander of the 8. Armee, Hitler visited the sector of Lodz which had surrendered without a fight. He visited a Luftwaffe unit, where a Hauptmann introduced him to the men. In the background, Himmler and Keitel. (ATB/USNA)

were separated from Hitler and they met him only a few times during the campaign in Poland.

The Führersonderzug arrived at Bad Polzin, Pomerania, at 1.56 a.m. on September 4. The Ministerzug (Ministers' Train), carrying von Ribbentrop and Himmler, arrived a quarter an hour later. The next day, the Führersonderzug moved to Plietnitz, south of Neustettin. Hitler, who had left earlier that morning in an automobile column to tour the 4. Armee area of operations, returned to Plietnitz in the evening.

On September 5, the train travelled north-west to Gross Born, south-west

Generalmajor Rommel, commander of the Führer-Begleit-Bataillon, Generalleutnant Karl-Heinrich Bodenschatz, Göring's liaison officer, and Hitler listened to the report by the local commander. (ATB/USNA)

On the 22nd, Hitler flew to Minsk-Mazowiecki, east of Warsaw, to hear a situation report from General der Artillerie Georg von Küchler, commander of the 3. Armee. In Glinki, he observed the besieged city through scissor binoculars. (ATB/USNA)

of Neustettin; on September 8 it moved far south to Ilnau, in Silesia, and on September 13 it was at Gogolin, south of Oppeln. Finally, on September 18 it was switched north again to Goddentow-Lanz, near Lauenburg in the north-east of Pomerania.

On September 19, the Führerhauptquartier transferred from the Führersonderzug, which remained at Goddentow-Lanz, to the Kasino Hotel in Zoppot, a few kilometres west of Danzig, where the FHQu set up till the 25th. From this base, as he had earlier from the Führersonderzug, Hitler visited the areas of military operations almost daily by automobile column or by air. Late in the afternoon of September 25, with all organised Polish resistance crushed, Hitler returned to his Sonderzug. Departing next morning, he returned at Berlin at 5.05 p.m. on September 26.

Along with Bormann and SS-Gruppenführer Dietrich, Reich Press Chief, Hitler inspected a destroyed Polish armoured train. (ATB/USNA)

THE BLITZKRIEG IN THE WEST, 1940

The Polish campaign quickly brought to light the limits of the Führersonderzug as a Führerhauptquartier. Even before the fighting ended, the construction of headquarters facilities in the West was discussed and on September 10, Hitler ordered a search to begin near the border with France to find a suitable location.

Alongside with Generalmajor Erwin Rommel, the commander of the Führer-Begleit-Bataillon, members of the search team were Oberst Rudolf Schmundt and Fritz Todt, head of the Organisation Todt. When travelling through the area they explored, they all wore civilian clothing.

The research resulted in three recommendations: the Ziegenberg Castle estate in the Taunus Mountains, an anti-aircraft position near the village of Rodert near Münstereifel, and a Westwall installation in the Kniebis Mountains near Freudenstadt. The decision finally went for the Ziegenberg Castle.

The actual construction of the Führerhauptquartiere was entrusted to the Organisation Todt and in September 1939 Siegfried Schmelcher was appointed Chefbaumeister der Führerhauptquartieranlagen (Senior Construction Engineer of the Führerhauptquartier Projects).

Construction work began at Ziegenberg estate at the end of September, with 100 workers, rapidly increasing to 1,900 in October and 3,400 in November.

Within the next month, work also began at the two other sites, in Rodert and near Freudenstadt. As if this was not enough, the Organisation Todt started building a fourth FHQu near Glan-Münchweiler in the Palatinate, which will soon be named 'Waldwiese'.

The simultaneous construction of four FHQu in the West from October 1939 to May 1940 certainly represented a waste of labour and materials.

FHQU 'MÜHLE'

In his report, Hauptbauleiter Schmelcher described the works as two individual complexes: 'Anlage Mühle' – after a disused water mill on the Usa River – near the Ziegenberg Castle and 'Anlage Wiesental' near the village of that name two kilometres north of the castle.

Works at 'Anlage Mühle' included fitting out the Ziegenberg Castle to provide 1,360 square metres for the FHQu, with three rooms on the ground floor for Hitler, whose servants, secretaries, and aides, as well as Keitel and Bormann, would occupy the upper floor. Catering and security staff occupied the basement, while 26 rooms for the rest of the staff were located upstairs immediately under the roof.

With the interior redevelopment of the castle being his responsibility, Speer spared no expense to provide Hitler with a living environment similar to that he had at Obersalzberg: wall panelling, walnut doors and window frames, designer furniture, new wallpaper and carpets, and paintings and sculptures for Hitler's living rooms.

The main work of Organisation Todt at 'Anlage Mühle' was the construction of five large work and accommodation bunkers with two-metre-thick concrete walls and ceilings. Stairs led from the castle porch to the first bunker with more than 20 work rooms arranged like railway compartments next to a through corridor. Long underground galleries – 300 linear metres in total – led from this bunker to three other bunkers of similar size, one providing work rooms and accommodation, the second housing communication equipment and the third signals installations and staff accommodation. In addition, two air-raid bunkers were built, and three air-raid shelters. The OT report states that 4,600 square metres of stone masonry was carried out to cover the walls of the bunkers. There was also a large car park, with a workshop and dormitory for drivers and mechanics, and two air-raid bunkers in the basement.

As for the Wiesental complex, Schmelcher reported the construction of seven single-story Massivhäuser with 50-centimetre-thick concrete walls and a 20-centimetre-thick concrete roof, the basements of each being an air-raid bunker with concrete walls and ceiling two metres or more thick. As at 'Anlage Mühle', extensive stone masonry was carried out to conceal the basement walls of the bunkers and Massivhäuser on the exposed side, and the facades of the upper floor of the latter were covered with woodwork. This, coupled with the overhanging wooden roofs, gave the buildings the appearance of country cottages.

South of the village, the Wachhaus was nearly 40 metres long. It housed Hitler's adjutants, secretaries, and maintenance staff, as well as his bodyguards. The six others Massivhäuser in the village averaged 26 to 28 metres long by 11 metres wide. Haus 1 was Hitler's house. It offered a large map room, a work room, a walnut panelled bedroom, a bathroom, and cloakroom. Additional rooms were intended for adjutants and servants, and Hitler's personal guards. From the corridor, a door led to Hitler's private quarters while a staircase of 36 steps led down to the anti-aircraft cellar.

Haus 2, known as Kasino, was the officers' mess. It was bordered lengthwise by a large terrace from which a covered walkway led to Hitler's House. Haus 3 was that of the OKW; Haus 4, the Generalhaus, was the residence of the generals; Haus 5 was the press house; Haus 6, the Reichsleiterhaus, was intended for party officials and ministers.

At Kransberg Castle nearby, 2,600 square metres were provided in Massivhäuser for the services of Reichsführer-SS Himmler.

In the middle of the 14th century, the Lords of Falkenstein built a castle in place of the old fortifications on a mountain spur above the hamlet of Ziegenberg. In 1939, the castle belonged to the von Schäffer-Bernstein family when it was confiscated by the Reich under the Sphere of Defence Act of 1935. Ziegenberg Castle, Then and Now. Partially restored after being destroyed by fighter-bombers in March 1945, the complex was transformed into condominiums in the early 1990s.
(Patrick Heil, Wikimedia Commons)

Other works included two communications stations and a series of anti-aircraft positions with 29 shelters and some 85 huts for gun crews. Road and trail work was also carried out, as well as camouflage work. Finally, the horticultural work consisted of moving and planting 2,160 trees and 33,000 shrubs, as well as sowing very large areas of lawn.

The Organisation Todt work for FHQu 'Felsennest' at Rodert (FHQu) and Hülloch (OKH) took a total of 85,500 working days. Most of the work was carried out at Hülloch, as evidenced by the usable surface area made available (680 square metres at Rodert, and 8,800 at Hülloch), and the volume of concrete used (3,000 cubic metres at Rodert and 5,500 at Hülloch).

The construction of 'Anlage Mühle' and 'Anlage Wiesental' took much longer than expected and when Oberstleutnant Kurt Thomas, the new commander of the FHQu, inspected the work with Rommel on January 22, 1940, they agreed that FHQu 'Ziegenberg' was far from ready.

In any case, when shown photographs of the Ziegenberg facilities

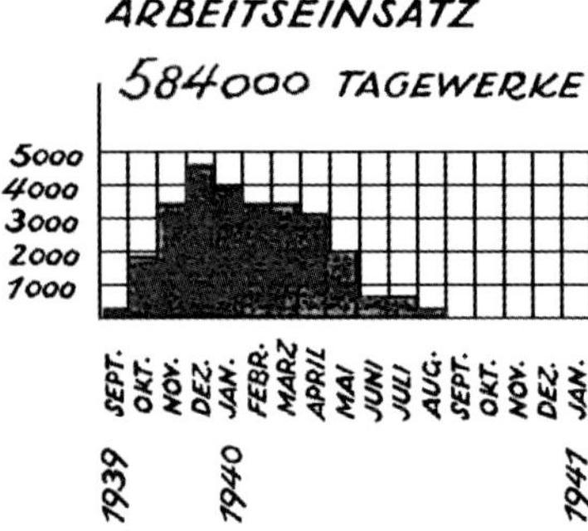

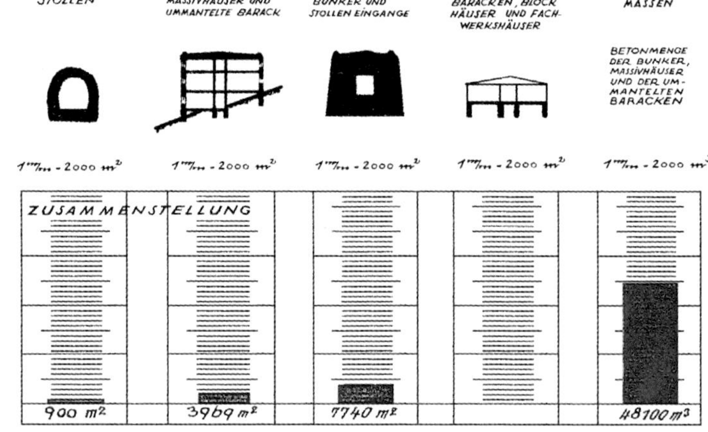

In November 1944, Siegfried Schmelcher, the Senior Construction Engineer of the Führerhauptquartier Projects at Organisation Todt (Chefbaumeister der Führerhauptquartieranlagen), filed a detailed report on the 16 Führer Headquarters which had by then been built, and of the three still under construction. This document of major importance was titled *Zusammenstellung der wichtigsten Daten über die von der OT gebauten Quartiere des Führers und der Wehrmachtteile* (Résumé of the most important data with respect to the HQs built by the OT for the Führer and the Wehrmacht arms of service). Schmelcher retained a copy of this report which only came to light when, before his death in 1991, he passed his papers to Professor Franz Seidler requesting that they be published. This came to fruition in 2000 when the professor, in conjunction with Dieter Zeigert, authored *Die Führerhauptquartiere 1939-1945.* The document is now available in the Bundesarchiv. The construction of FHQu 'Mühle' at Ziegenberg and Wiesental appears as number 1 in the Schmelcher's report. This sketch describes the workforce engaged in the construction from September 1939 through August 1940, a peak of 4,500 workers being reached in December 1939. The work required a total of 584,000 working days, more than two third of which were for 'Anlage Mühle'.

According to this report, the works provided some 11,700 square metres of useful space for the FHQu, of which 7,740 square metres were in heavy bunkers and 3,969 square metres in 'Ummantelte Baracken'. Of the latter figure, 2,609 square metres were at Kransberg Castle for the services of the Reichsführer-SS. The figures on the left column are for tunnels dug out or fitted out, 900 square metres in this case. The second column refers to the 'Ummantelte Baracken', wooden huts clad with a 30-60 centimetres thick concrete shell within 10-30 centimetres of the walls and having a concrete ceiling. Steel plates four centimetres thick could be bolted over the windows for splinter protection and the entrances had two-winged doors of two centimetres thick steel. These 'Massivhäuser' were only 'splittersicher' – shrapnel proof. The figures in the third column refer to heavy bunkers and the fourth to wooden huts – prefabricated, single-storey, delivered on site for assembly on concrete foundations – and other constructions. These four columns give figures in square metres. The column on the right gives, in cubic metres, the total amount of concrete used, 48,100 cubic metres. Of these, 38,000 were used for the work at 'Anlage Mühle', and just over 10,000 for the work at 'Anlage Wiesental'.

in February 1940, Hitler objected and made it clear that he had no intention of using such 'luxurious' accommodation during a campaign when soldiers were fighting. On the 22nd, he decided to establish his FHQu in the more spartan 'Felsennest' to conduct the offensive in the West in May 1940.

The Ziegenberg complex had a second chance in July 1940 when Hitler issued his Directive No. 16 detailing the directions for Operation 'Seelöwe', the invasion of England. The directive designated the complex as the Führer's headquarters for this operation and demanded that from August 1, 'the operations staffs of the commanders in chief of the Army, the Navy, and the Luftwaffe must be within the area with a maximum radius of 50 kilometres from my headquarters at Ziegenberg.'

As early as June 29, an advance detachment of the Führer-Begleit-Bataillon left FHQu 'Tannenberg', where Hitler had just settled, in order

None of the photographs that may have been taken at 'Anlage Mühle' or 'Anlage Wiesental' appear to have survived the war. Located on the side of the road leading to Wiesental, the garage block survived the war unscathed and was taken over by the American occupation forces until the late 1990s. The building was then converted into office accomodation.

Just north of Ziegenberg, on the side of the road leading to Wiesental, Haus VII still stands, which shows the stone masonry that conceals the basement walls of the bunker and the woodwork covering the facades of the upper floor. (Boris Roessler)

Wanting all new buildings of the Third Reich to serve as an example for future generations, Dr. Todt demanded that they be aesthetically and architecturally perfect monuments. It is not surprising that after being shown photographs of these constructions, Hitler found the site too luxurious and decided to settle instead in the more spartan 'Felsennest'. (Helius FFM)

to establish security preparations at Ziegenberg. On July 5, the rest of the Führer-Begleit-Bataillon moved to Ziegenberg, along with a 600-man Luftwaffe anti-aircraft detachment. Operation 'Seelöwe' was then postponed, and the Führer-Begleit-Bataillon left the area in November and the IX. Armeekorps in Kassel took over the Ziegenberg compound.

A document drawn up in the autumn of 1944 by the Führer-

Nachrichtenabteilung, the telecommunications unit of the FHQu, indicates that 'Amt 600', the code name for the Ziegenberg and Wiesental complex, was not ready to be occupied and used as, if cables were laid, telecommunications equipment was not available.

In October, that the headquarters complex was used by Ob. West, the headquarters of the Commander-in-Chief West, Generalfeldmarschall Gerd von Rundstedt.

FHQU 'FELSENNEST'

On October 1, 1939, work began on the construction of FHQu 'Felsennest' on the Eselsberg hill just south-west of Rodert. The work was not given a specific name but took over the existing topographic name of the mountain ridge, Felsennest.

In his report, Schmelcher mentions that the complex consisted of two parts, the FHQu complex at Rodert and the OKH complex at Hülloch, five kilometres to the east. Work ran in parallel at both sites until March 31, 1940, when work at Hülloch was completed, and work at Rodert continued until May 10.

At Rodert, the Organisation Todt built four bunkers with a usable surface area of 250 square metres, two concrete-reinforced buildings with a usable surface of 130 square metres, and three wooden huts of 300 square metres. The work also included camouflage work, the remodelling of five houses in the village and work on the road from Münstereifel to Rodert.

On the hill above Rodert, Sperrkreis I (Security Zone I) was encircled by a

The heaviest construction within Sperrkreis I at Rodert was the Führer's bunker (on the right in this photo). Just near by, the Lagebaracke (left), a hut-type building where the situation conferences were held. Both were hidden by a large sloping camouflage cover with a door through it to access the Führer's bunker and another door (not seen here) to access the Lagebaracke.

The small terrace in front of the Lagebaracke seen from inside the camouflage cover, and the entrance (right).

Another view from inside the camouflage awning, looking out through the open door. An SS-Obersturmführer takes a break in front of the Lagebaracke. Note the 'K-Stand' sign. (ATB/USNA)

chain-link fence overlooked at intervals by wooden guard towers perched on tall wooden legs. The heaviest construction of the six within Sperrkreis I was the Führer's bunker, which was small. There was also a building for the adjutants, and the Lagebaracke, a hut-type building where the situation conferences were held.

The Lagebaracke map room, and Hitler's living room. These photographs clearly show that FHQu 'Felsennest' was simple and therefore in accordance with Hitler's wishes.

An SS-Untersturmführer of the Führer-Begleit-Kommando stands guard at the entrance to the Lagebaracke. Note the 'Adolf Hitler' cuff title. The steep slope of the camouflage gives a peculiar appearance to this entrance. (ATB/USNA)

The other parts of the Führerhauptquartier were in Sperrkreis II, dispersed in the village of Rodert, including Oberst Walter Warlimont's Abteilung Landesverteidigung, or Abteilung L (National Defence Branch, the most important group within the Wehrmachtführungsstab).

In Hülloch, seven bunkers were built for the OKH to provide 800 square metres of usable space. In addition, 30 wooden huts were built, the Haniel forest lodge was adapted to this new use, and camouflage and road improvement works were carried out.

On February 22, Hitler chose the 'Felsennest' to be his FHQu during the coming offensive against France and in mid-March, the first units of the Führer-Begleit-Bataillon arrived in Rodert to guard the installations.

Men from Himmler's personal staff chatted through the windows of the Lagebaracke's map room. Note the SS-Standartenführer in the centre and the cuff title 'RFSS' worn by the SS-Obersturmführer on the right. The sign at the top left signalled a Luftschutzraum (air raid shelter) and its capacity of 40 people. The efficient German administration has made a mailbox (Feldpost) available to users, even in the heart of a high security headquarters. (ATB/USNA)

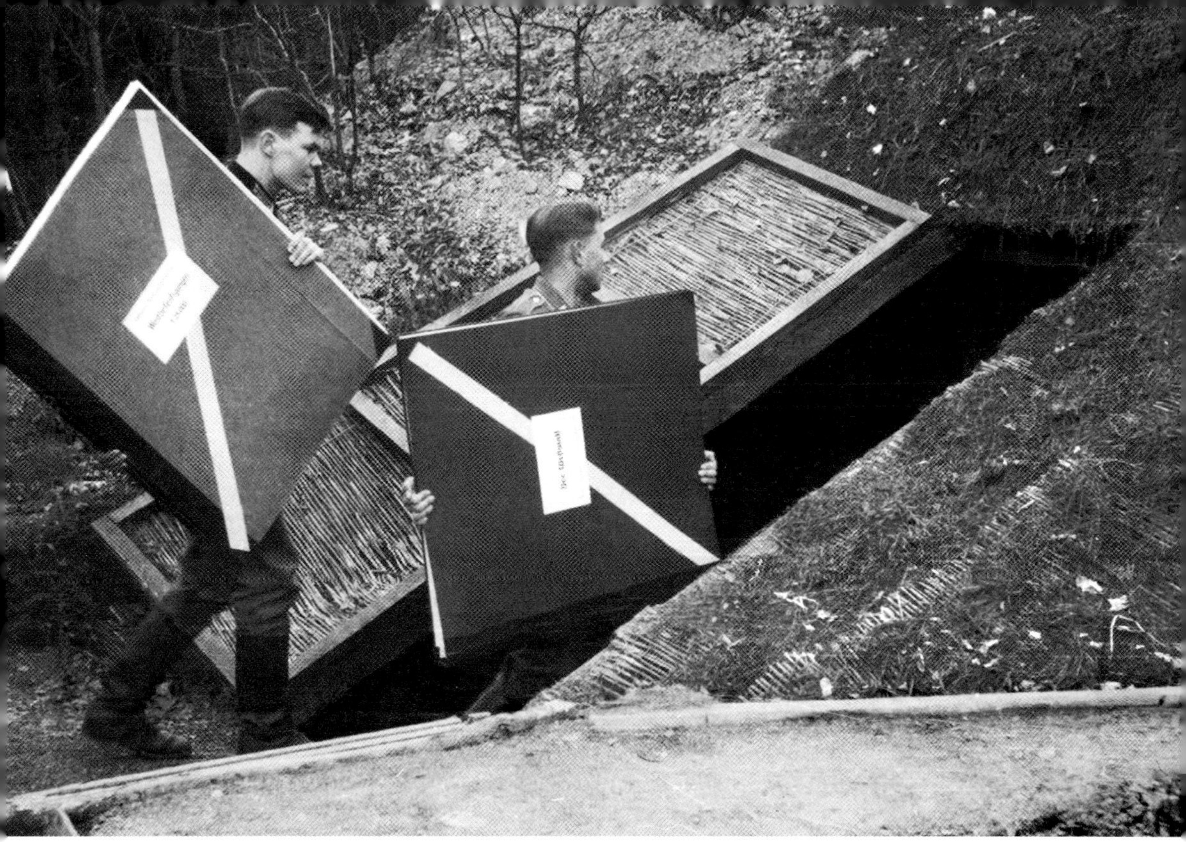

Before a situation conference, assistants brought two large files into the Lagebaracke. Remarkably, the label on the cover tells us what it was: Westbefestigungen (fortifications in the West), and the Westwall. (ATB/USNA)

Alighted from the Sonderzug in Euskirchen, Hitler arrived on May 10 at 5 a.m. at the FHQu 'Felsennest'. Bormann, Keitel and von Below were with him in the 'three-axle' Mercedes. Five minutes behind arrived the vehicles carrying Dietrich, Hoffmann, Schmundt and the secretaries. A third convoy transported the baggage.

This photograph of his Mercedes driving down Waldstrasse in Rodert in this direction actually shows a departure from the FHQu. Rodert.

Waldstrasse today.

Early on May 10, Führersonderzug 'Amerika', as it was now called, brought Hitler to Euskirchen station. Met there by a detachment of the Führer-Begleit-Bataillon, he proceeded in automobile column and arrived at 5.00 a.m. at FHQu 'Felsennest'. The Führersonderzug then went on to park on a siding in Heusenstamm, south-east of Frankfurt-am-Main.

Foreign Minister von Ribbentrop, Reichsführer-SS Himmler and Reich Chancellery Chief Hans Lammers were on the 'Heinrich' train stationed at Flammersfeld near Altenkirchen. Göring's 'Asien' train was located near a railway tunnel at Trimbs, south-east of Mayen.

The German attack on France began at 5.35 a.m. on May 10, half an hour after Hitler's arrival at FHQu 'Felsennest'.

On May 11, Hitler visited the OKH headquarters at Hülloch, his only visit to the OKH during the campaign in the West. On May 13, he received at 'Felsennest' the paratroopers who had just assaulted the Belgian fort of Eben-Emael and awarded them the Knight's Cross.

In the early hours of May 10, German airborne troops stormed the Belgian fortress at Eben-Emael, landing in gliders on the fort's roof. The 'impregnable' Fort Eben-Emael fell in just 28 hours. On May 13, nine members of the assault group were invited to FHQu 'Felsennest' to receive the Knight's Cross. First, the nine men were introduced to Hitler. (ATB/USNA)

Then Hitler presented the Knight's Cross to each of them, starting with Hauptmann Walter Koch, the group's leader. (ATB/USNA)

The place was already overgrown and hardly recognisable when Winston Ramsey, the founder of *After the Battle*, visited the site in 1977. He was unsuccessful in finding this location and eventually spoke to a local farmer who told him that this track had been completely obliterated when new gravel paths were laid in 1974. This was the comparison of the same spot. (ATB/USNA)

The paratroopers were then invited to chat with the FHQu staff in front of the Lagebaracke. Here Koch presented his award document to Hauptmann von Below, Hitler's Luftwaffe Adjutant. (ATB/USNA)

Generalmajor Jodl and his adjutant, Major Willy Deyhle, chatted with the paratroopers. (ATB/USNA)

Generalleutnant Bodenschatz, Göring's liaison officer with Hitler, admired the Knight's Cross hanging at Koch's neck. In the background were Oberleutnant Otto Zierach and Oberleutnant Gustav Altmann. (ATB/USNA)

Hitler chatted with Leutnant Joachim Meissner, Oberleutnant Witzig, and Hauptmann Koch. (ATB/USNA)

After decorating the nine Fallschirmjägers, Hitler posed in their midst in front of the Lagebaracke (see the bottom corner of the door in the slanted camouflage on the edge of the photo on the right). First row, from left to right: Leutnant Egon Delica, Hauptmann Walter Koch, Hitler, Leutnant Joachim Messner, and Oberleutnant Gustav Altmann. Second row: Oberleutnant Rudolf Witzig, Oberleutnant Otto Zierach, Leutnant Helmut Ringler, Oberleutnant Walter Kiess, and Oberarzt Dr. Rolf Jäger. (ATB/USNA)

On May 17, he flew from Odendorf, the 'Felsennest' airfield north-east of Münstereifel, to visit Generalfeldmarschall von Rundstedt, the commander of Heeresgruppe A then located at Bastogne. On May 24, he visited von

In her book *He Was My Chief* published in 1985, Christa Schroeder, one of Hitler's secretaries, described how he was enraptured by the beautiful scenery and the woods filled with birdsong. She noted that he never spent as much time outdoors as he did at 'Felsennest'. Here in company with Hauptmann von Below and SS-Oberführer Hewel at the entrance of the Lagebaracke. (ATB/USNA)

From the beginning of the offensive in the West, the daily routine at FHQu revolved around two situation conferences at the Lagebaracke, the principal at midday, followed by a shorter session of updates in the evening. Hitler discusses the situation in the conference room with Jodl and Keitel, and Major Deyhle. (ATB/USNA)

Rundstedt again, by then at Charleville, and sanctioned the famous 'Halt Order' proposed by the Army Group. The German forces stopped for three days in the Dunkirk sector, which gave the Allies time to organise the evacuation and build a defensive line.

'Felsennest' headquarters, May 25. Hitler on the telephone in the Lagebaracke, Bormann in attendance, with (standing in the background) SS-Obersturmführer Hans-Georg Schulze and SS-Obersturmführer Hans Pfeiffer, Hitler's ordnance officer, and SS-Gruppenführer Otto Dietrich, Reich Press Chief. (ATB/USNA)

The weather remained sunny throughout May 1940, with only one day of rain on the 29th, and Hitler and FHQu staff spent a lot of time outside. General der Artillerie Friedrich Fromm, Chief of Army Equipment and commander of the Replacement Army, reports to Hitler. Major Engel is between them and Oberst Schmundt is hidden by Fromm. (ATB/USNA)

SS-Gruppenführer Schaub, Hitler's personal adjutant, Oberst Schmundt, Hitler and Bormann. In the background, SS-Obersturmführer Schulze and SS-Obersturmführer Pfeiffer. (ATB/USNA)

On May 21, Hitler spoke with some of his inner circle in front of the Lagebaracke. Seated, from left to right, Bormann, Hoffmann and Hitler. Standing in the middle, SS-Obersturmbannführer Brandt, Hitler's escort doctor; standing on the right, Fregattenkapitän Karl Jesko Puttkammer, Kriegsmarine Adjutant. (ATB/USNA)

Himmler, who was, with von Ribbentrop and Reich Chancellery Chief Lammers, on the 'Heinrich' train stationed near Altenkirchen, visited FHQu 'Felsennest' on several occasions. Another view from inside the camouflage awning, of Himmler speaking with Arthur Seyss-Inquart. Outside, Hitler was speaking with Richard Walther Darré. (ATB/USNA)

One of the leading Nazi 'blood and soil' ideologues, Darré was Minister of Food and Agriculture. After the war, he was to be tried at Nuremberg as one of 21 defendants in the Ministries Trial, and was sentenced to seven years in prison. (ATB/USNA)

A bench was installed at the junction of tracks in front of the Lagebaracke and the place became the agora where everyone at 'Felsennest' met and chatted. Keitel spoke with Seyss-Inquart, the governor of Ostmark, the name given to Austria when it became part of the Third Reich. (ATB/USNA)

Then Himmler conferred with Seyss-Inquart in company with SS-Gruppenführer Gottlob Berger, Chief of the SS Main Office. They were probably discussing the upcoming appointment of Seyss-Inquart as Reich Commissioner for the occupied Netherlands. After the war, facing trial at Nuremberg, Seyss-Inquart was convicted of war crimes and crimes against humanity. Sentenced to death, he was hanged in October 1946. (ATB/USNA)

Subordinates relaxed in the same place. Women secretaries are very rarely seen in photos taken at the FHQu. It seems that these two ladies were Christa Schroeder and Gerda Daranowski. (ATB/USNA)

Göring, whose 'Asien' train was stationed at Trimbs, south-east of Mayen, also visited 'Felsennest'. (ATB/USNA)

Hitler, who later referred to 'Felsennest' as his nicest FHQu, took long walks on the hill. Here he was walking down to Rodert in company with SA-Obergruppenführer Brückner, Hauptmann von Below, Oberst Schmundt and SS-Obersturmführer Schulze, when a plane appeared in the sky. Although they did not seem particularly worried, it seems like they were not sure if this plane was friend or foe. (ATB/USNA)

Exploring the 'Felsennest' hill in 1977, Winston Ramsey had great difficulty finding this location until a local farmer showed him where the old road obliterated in 1974 had been. One of the new gravel paths is just visible behind the original one in this comparison. (ATB/USNA)

Hitler and Oberst Schmundt led the walk down to Rodert. The main Sperrkreis I gate to the Führerhauptquartier can be seen in the distance. In 1977, all but this short stretch of the old road was completely obliterated. (ATB/USNA)

Once the farmer had pointed out the line of the original road, everything fell into place. Winston Ramsey chose this comparison which does not exactly match the photo of Hitler's party coming down the hill, but shows both the new path and the old. (ATB/USNA)

Major Engel walks at Hitler's right, behind Engel's right shoulder is SS-Obersturmführer Schulze, and Hauptmann von Below is behind Hitler's left shoulder. This stretch of the old road has been completely obliterated. (ATB/USNA)

The party passed through the Sperrkreis I gate, and then reached Rodert. SA-Obergruppenführer Brückner is behind Hitler's left shoulder, and Oberst Schmundt walks at Hitler's left. (ATB/USNA)

On June 1, Hitler and his entourage undertook a two-day trip in an automobile column, travelling through southern Belgium and northern France. They visited Army and Corps commanders as well as First World War sites. They spent the night from June 1 to 2 at the Château de Brigode in Annappes near Lille and returned to 'Felsennest' on the 2nd.

Hitler left 'Felsennest' on June 6 to settle in FHQu 'Wolfsschlucht' in Brûly-de-Pesche. In November 1940, the complex was transferred to the Army.

A document produced in the autumn of 1944 by the Führer-

Vimy Canadian Memorial, Then and Now. On June 2 morning, General der Infanterie Hermann Hoth, commander of the V. Armeekorps, briefed Hitler and his party on the terrace of the memorial. In the background, the figure of 'Canada in Mourning' was still covered by the wooden shuttering built by the French to protect it from being damaged in the battle.

In the afternoon, the motorcade reached Bouchain where the crossings of the Escaut river had been hotly contested just a few days before. General der Artillerie Walter Heitz, commander of the VIII. Armeekorps, took Hitler and his party to the top of the 12th century Ostrevant tower and described the battle from this vantage point. The party returned to 'Felsennest' in the evening.

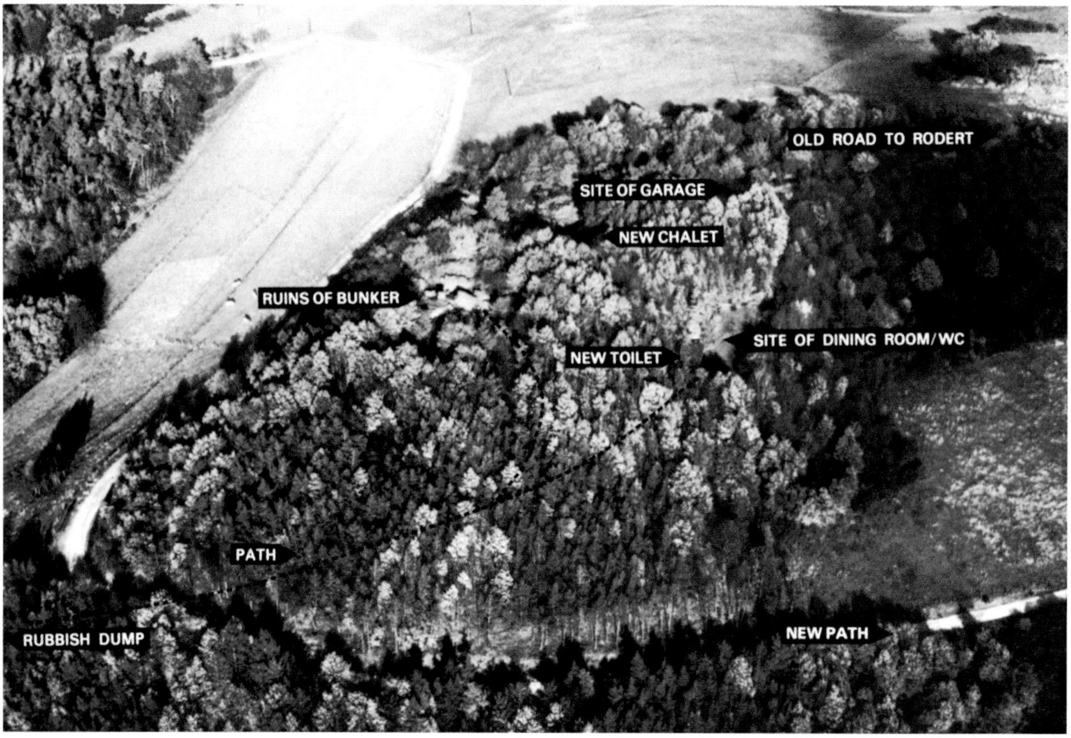

To illustrate the confusing situation of the old trails that have disappeared and the new trails that have been traced, *After the Battle* had this aerial photograph taken in November 1977 of the overgrown 'Felsennest' hill. In the 1970s, the name 'Felsennest' was removed from the official topographic map and replaced by 'Eselsberg'.

Nachrichtenabteilung listed 'WO', the codename then in use for the complex at Rodert, as one of the four FHQu that were ready for occupation and use as regards to their telecommunications installations. In September, the 7. Armee established its headquarters in the installations around the Hülloch forest lodge, followed at the end of November by Generalfeldmarschall

The FHQu installations on the 'Felsennest' hill were destroyed by German engineers at the beginning of March 1945 and American troops occupied the sector on March 7. American troops examine the ruins of the blown bunker on 'Felsennest' hill. In 1977, *After the Battle* discovered that the blasted concrete remains were largely as they were in 1945. (USNA)

Walter Model, commanding Heeresgruppe B, who led the Ardennes offensive from here.

The installations were destroyed by German engineers at the beginning of March 1945 and the GIs took Münstereifel and its surroundings on March 7, without a fight.

FHQU 'WOLFSSCHLUCHT'

As the Wehrmacht's advance proceeded at a rapid pace, Hitler pushed to move his Führerhauptquartier further west, closer to the action. On May 19, a sector of the French fortifications east of Avesnes was investigated for this purpose but was ultimately rejected because the bunker that had been selected proved unsuitable.

Three days later, the small Belgian village of Brûly-de-Pesche, a few kilometres from the French border, was chosen and the population of all the neighbouring villages was evacuated; in fact, many residents had already

As the Wehrmacht advanced deeper into France, it was decided to move the Führerhauptquartier closer to the action and on May 22, the small village of Brûly-de-Pesche in southern Belgium was chosen. The inhabitants who remained were evacuated, and the Organisation Todt began to convert the ten-farmhouse village into FHQu 'Wolfsschlucht'. Organisation Todt workmen dig a trench in preparation for the laying of communication cables.

These photos were taken in the last days of May (reporting later on the construction of FHQu 'Wolfsschlucht', Schmelcher indicated that work at Brûly-de-Pesche started on May 25). Spools of communication cable were unloaded in front of the latrine building behind the school house. (ATB and Google)

left, having fled the advancing German armies (all Belgians remembered the numerous cases of civilians murdered by German troops in August 1914).

Reporting later on the construction of FHQu 'Wolfsschlucht', Schmelcher indicated that it was built from May 25 to June 6, with a workforce of 600 men, for a total of 7,200 days of work.

The work provided 25 square metres of useful space in a small bunker for Hitler and 1,500 square metres in wooden huts. Schmelcher noted in his report that there were five huts, the one for Hitler was near the bunker and another nearby, known as Kasino, was the officers' mess. Ten houses in the village were reinforced and reconfigured (classified as 'Massivhäuser'

Arrows painted on the water trough directed arriving workers to the Organisation Todt office in the village. The house in the background would soon house the press services of the FHQu and the OT would call it 'Wolfspalast'. The pump and the trough are still there today, just out of the photo on the left in this comparison. (ATB and Google)

Ernst Vollbehr, an official painter, shows with this painting the arrangement of buildings in the dense forest just north of the village: Hitler's hut is under his brush on the left, the bunker is on the right and the Saint-Méen fountain in the centre. Already known for his landscape and WW1 paintings, Vollbehr painted pictures of Nazi Party rallies and of the Berlin's Olympic facilities in the 1930s. Fritz Todt commissioned paintings from him representing the construction of the Reich's highways, and Vollbehr became one of Germany's most popular artists. He painted pictures during the invasion of Poland in 1939 and, as seen here, during the campaign in the West. Vollbehr created an enormous body of work, with thousands of paintings.

Compared to the 'luxurious' works invested for FHQu 'Ziegenberg' (over 48,000 cubic metres of concrete) and the reasonable 'Felsennest' (8,500 cubic metres of concrete), FHQu 'Wolfsschlucht' was a modest work using only 630 cubic metres of concrete. Only 25 square metres of useful space were provided in the bunker.

The Führerhauptquartier staff moved from 'Felsennest' on June 6 and Hitler arrived at Brûly at 1.30 p.m. At the entrance of the village, he chatted with headquarters personnel in front of the house occupied by the FHQu press services. The Organisation Todt named the house 'Wolfspalast' in a reference to Hitler's cover name 'Herr Wolf' in the early days of the Nazi Party. The house is today the welcome place for the 'Brûly-de-Pesche 1940' visits, with a cafeteria and an exhibition room telling the history of the Brigade Piron, a unit of the Free Belgian Forces which fought in the side of the Allies. (ATB and Google)

Hitler went to greet Göring who had just landed in a Storch light aircraft on the airstrip set up on a meadow just south of the village.

by Schmelcher) to provide an additional 800 square metres, and the village school was appropriated for the situation room. Additionally, roads and bridges were built and camouflage work was carried out.

A landing strip for Fieseler Storch light aircraft was cleared on a meadow just south of the village.

The OKH was located in Forges, a small village about 15 kilometres north-west of Brûly-de-Pesche, as well as in Chimay and the neighbouring hamlets. In Chimay, the Organisation Todt requisitioned and reinforced 25 houses, which Schmelcher classified as 'Massivhäuser', thus providing 2,000 square metres of usable space.

Operation 'Rot', the second phase of the German offensive in the West, begun on June 5 and the Führerhauptquartier staff moved from 'Felsennest' on June 6. Hitler departed by air and arrived at FHQu 'Wolfsschlucht' at 1.30 p.m.

On June 16, he was driven by car to the Château d'Acoz, southeast of Charleroi, to meet General Juan Vigón, chief-of-staff of the Spanish Armed Forces. The next morning, the French government requested, through Spain, armistice conditions.

The French request was received at the Foreign Office in Berlin and was immediately forwarded to Walther Hewel, von Ribbentrop's envoy to the Führerhauptquartier. Cameraman Walter Frentz captured the precise moment when Hewel happily passed the information to Hitler. Delighted, he

Hitler and Göring, and some of the inner circle, stretch their legs in front of the church. Hitler's bunker and hut, and the Kasino hut (officers' club), were in the woods in the left background. (ATB/USNA)

Studying positions and movements on a map of France, with Hess, Bormann, and Keitel on June 16. On the extreme right is SS-Hauptsturmführer Max Wünsche, Hitler's orderly officer.

Hitler, whose poor eyesight was not publicised, uses a magnifying glass to mark a detail on a situation map. On the right is SS-Obergruppenführer Karl Wolff, Himmler's liaison officer.

'The Führer discusses the next operations in the FHQu', was the original caption of this propaganda photo. Generaloberst Keitel, Major Willy Deyhle, General Jodl, Hitler, Generaloberst von Brauchitsch and Admiral Raeder at 'Wolfsschlucht'.

On June 10 Italy declared war on France and Great Britain, and Hitler issued a proclamation stating that 'At this hour all Germany is filled with jubilation that Fascist Italy, of her own free will, has entered the struggle against the common enemy, France and Great Britain, on our side.'

Göring, who stayed in his Sonderzug 'Asien' during the campaign, often visited 'Wolfsschlucht', using the Storch landing field just south of 'Wolfspalast'. Note how many trees had had white blackout ring painted. (ATB/USNA)

Eye-witness accounts state that Hitler spent most of his time in the open air at 'Wolfsschlucht' because the buildings were infested with midges and the recently applied varnish made his eyes swell. Hitler and Keitel stroll near the Saint-Méen fountain, Hitler's hut in the background. (ATB/USNA)

On 14 June, Hitler conferred with Himmler in the open air near the Saint-Méen fountain. Note the secretary heading towards her office in the hut, an unusual sight for female secretaries who are rarely seen in photos taken at the FHQu. (ATB/USNA)

Himmler examines documents with SA-Obergruppenführer Wilhelm Brückner, Hitler's Chief adjutant. Note the 'Adolf Hitler' cuff title worn by the SS-Obersturmführer on the right. (ATB/USNA)

Himmer's driver, SS-Obersturmführer Hans Bastians, was waiting for the conference to end when his Schmeisser MP 38, a sub-machine gun known as dangerous with its safety in the open bolt position, accidently discharged. Fatally wounded in the head, Bastians was buried in the village that day. His grave was since reburied at Lommel Soldatenfriedhof, Belgium, Block 5, Grave 136.

Hitler, Keitel, Bormann, Ministerialrat Wilfrid Bade, Gauleiter Adolf Wagner, and von Ribbentrop. Bade was a ministerial official of the Reich Ministry of Public Enlightenment and Propaganda of Josef Goebbels and Gauleiter Wagner was Reich Defence Commissioner for Military Districts VII and XIII. (ATB/USNA)

Study of a report in the open air and impromptu conference near the Saint-Méen fountain. Hitler, Bormann, Rudolf Hess, the Deputy Führer (Stellvertreter des Führers), and Brückner. In the left background we can see the facade of the church. (ATB/USNA)

Hitler, Keitel, von Ribbentrop, Walther Hewell, von Ribbentrop's liaison officer with Hitler, and Bormann. (ATB/USNA)

Major Engel and Oberst Schmundt comment a map, Major Deyhle and SS-Obergruppenführer Wolff, Himmler's liaison officer with Hitler, looks on. (ATB/USNA)

Brückner addresses some of the inner circle at the table near the Saint-Méen fountain. Among them, Heinrich Hoffmann (fourth from left, looking at the photographer) and SS-Obersturmbannführer Karl Brandt. We have often seen Brückner at Brûly-de-Pesche, and previously at FHQu 'Wolfsschlucht', but we will not see him in the rest of this book: Bormann's intrigues to sideline him ultimately succeeded and in October 1940 Brückner was replaced as Chief adjutant by SS-Gruppenführer Julius Schaub. Brückner then joined the army and became a colonel at the end of the war. (ATB/USNA)

raised his right leg and stamped his foot sharply. Cleverly rigged by John Grierson, this brief scene will become the 'Führer jig', a great moment of propaganda for the Allies.

Later that day (June 17) Hitler flew to Frankfurt, and, boarding Führersonderzug 'Amerika', arrived in Munich at noon on June 18 for consultation with Mussolini. He then returned to FHQu 'Wolfsschlucht' at 2.15 p.m. on June 19.

On June 21, 1940, Hitler was driven by car to the Compiègne forest, north-east of Paris. There, in the same railway car used for the capitulation of Germany to the Western Allies in 1918, France had to sign the armistice. Showing disdain, Hitler stayed only for the reading of the document's preamble by Generaloberst Keitel and he was back at 'Wolfsschlucht' by 8.00 p.m.

At 1 a.m. on June 17, the French government requested, through Spain, armistice conditions. The French request was received at the Foreign Office in Berlin and forwarded to Walther Hewel, von Ribbentrop's envoy to the Führerhauptquartier. Hewel passed the information to Hitler in the morning. (ATB/USNA)

Cameraman Walter Frentz captured the precise moment. Delighted to hear the news, Hitler raised his right leg and lowered it abruptly, tapping his foot in the process. When this film was released outside Germany, John Grierson, commissioner of the National Film Board of Canada, thought he could do a great propaganda job with it. By looping and duplicating the relevant footage, he managed to transform the incident into the 'Führer jig', thus making Hitler appear somewhat ridiculous in Western newsreels. Grierson exposed his trick in Esquire magazine in 1958.

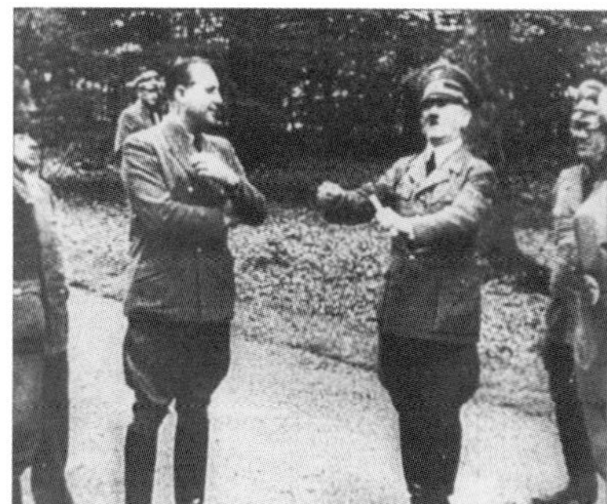

Having left 'Wolfsschlucht' by car at 11.30 a.m. on June 22, Hitler arrived at Compiègne at 3.15 p.m. The German delegation was waiting for him: From left to right: Hess, von Ribbentrop, Admiral Raeder (shaking hands with Hitler), Göring, and von Brauchitsch. In the background, the Alsace-Lorraine statue has been draped with German flags to cover the stone image of the German eagle being stabbed by the Allied golden sword.

At Rethondes, in the same railway car used for the capitulation of Germany to the Western Allies in 1918, France had to sign the armistice.

Many members of his usual entourage accompanied Hitler on his lighting tour of Paris on June 23: Keitel, Brückner, Schaub, Dietrich, Bodenschatz, Schmundt, and Engel. Also present were two architects, Albert Speer and Hermann Giesler, and the sculptor Arno Breker, who were knowledgeable about the architectural history of Paris and had prepared an itinerary to take in all the important monuments. However, Hitler knew the French capital very well from his study of maps and books and claimed that he would be able to navigate the streets without a guide. The party stopped at the Trocadéro and Hitler posed in well known photos with his back to the Tour Eifel.

The whistle-stop continued via the Invalides and Montmartre where they stopped to admire the city bathed in sunshine. Generaloberst Keitel (left), Hitler, Speer, Giesler, and Breker, SS-Hauptsturmführer Wünsche.

Hitler departed from 'Wolfsschlucht' by air at 4.05 a.m. on June 23 to visit Paris and, after a whirlwind tour of the city, returned to Brûly by 10.30 a.m. the same day.

On June 25 and 26, Hitler set off again in an automobile column to revisit places he had known during the First World War. Max Amann and Ernst Schmied, two of his comrades in that conflict, joined the usual entourage for these travels. Then, with Hitler wanting to visit the battlefields of the First World War in Alsace, as well as the fortifications of the Maginot Line, it was decided to move the FHQu to the 'Tannenberg' facilities in the Black Forest.

Departing by air at 8.00 a.m. on June 28 from Gros-Caillou, about fifteen kilometres south of Brûly, he flew to Eutingen, east of Freudenstadt.

The Germans immediately abandoned 'Wolfsschlucht', after having recovered the communications equipment and dismantled the wooden huts. Frames, windows, and doors, as well as fixtures and fittings, were all taken away for use at other sites. The Organisation Todt also rebuilt the church tower which they had dismantled in May.

The residents, most of whom had been evacuated to villages north of Couvin, about ten kilometres away, began to return in the first days of July.

Only the small bunker remained standing in the wood, and neither the Germans nor the Americans thought of destroying it. In the post-war years, the owner of the forest considered removing it, but friends and local personalities advised him against doing so, emphasizing its historical interest.

In the 1960s a local historian, Mr. André Georges, began to collect information about the former FHQu, notably by tracing and questioning Germans who were there in June 1940.

In the early 1990s it was decided to revive the site as a historic place and in 1993 two wooden huts were rebuilt, one on the site where was Hitler's one

On the night of June 24-25, as the cease-fire was about to come into effect at 12.35 a.m. (the armistice has been signed on June 22), Hitler and the FHQu staff listen to the radio announcement of the armistice with France in the Kasino hut.

and one on the site where was the officers' mess.

'Brûly-de-Pesche 1940' now manages visits to the site, and the two huts house exhibitions telling the history of the FHQu in 1940, and of the Resistance assembled in a nearby forest in 1944. We invite you to consult their website https://bdp1940.be/.

Then, from four positions around the FHQu, buglers sounded 'Ganze Halt' (Cease Fire). In the mess, everyone stood to attention in complete silence. As the notes died away, Keitel said a few words and three cheers went up in honour of the Führer, the Supreme Commander of the Armed Forces. Hitler sat in silence for a minute or so, stood up and then left. Giesler and Breker were present and both later testified that they had seen tears in Hitler's eyes.

FHQU 'TANNENBERG'

Anlage 'Tannenberg' was established as an adaptation and expansion of existing facilities of the Air Defence on the edge of a moor-like clearing on the Black Forest High Road from Freudenstadt to Baden-Baden.

Schmelcher reported that Anlage 'Tannenberg' was built for 'parts only of the FHQu' between October 1939 and June 1940, with a peak of 500 workers in November and December. The work took a total of 43,750 working days and used the small amount of 2,340 cubic metres of concrete.

The work provided 275 square metres of usable space in two bunkers, one bunker was to serve as Hitler's living quarters, while the other housed a telecommunications centre. A wooden hut of 85 square metres was erected, and some of the existing buildings were developed. Oberst Warlimont's

Hitler resided at FHQu 'Tannenberg' from June 26 to July 6. During his stay he and his entourage remained in the open most of the time. The bunker's concrete was not yet dry and Hitler later said 'if we had stayed any length of time there, we would all have gone down with something.' Hitler strolls with Baldur von Schirach, Hitler Youth Leader, and von Ribbentrop in a typical Black Forest setting. (ATB/USNA)

They met guests at the main junction of tracks in the compound, note the bridge over the ditch. New fir trees and thick snow covered the entire site when *After the Battle* visited the former FHQu in 1977 but the Editor managed to uncover a former pathway. (ATB/USNA)

Abteilung Landesverteidigung was located in the Hotel Alexanderschanze, over one kilometre away from the FHQu.

Hitler arrival was announced by a visit of Generalmajor Schmundt, senior Wehrmacht adjutant, and Oberstleutnant Thomas, commander of the FHQu, on June 16. On the 25th, the WFSt staff left FHQu 'Wolfsschlucht' in a motor convoy and drove to 'Tannenberg' via Sedan and Strasbourg, crossing the Rhine at Kehl. Hitler himself arrived by plane on June 28 and landed at Eutingen, east of Freudenstadt. He was then driven to Anlage 'Tannenberg', where he arrived at 11.00 a.m.

He expressed his satisfaction that the FHQu was as simple as he wished and in the afternoon he toured Alsace in an automobile column, visiting Strasbourg and meeting General Friedrich Dollmann, commander of the 7. Armee. He returned to Alsace on the 30th to inspect casemates of the Maginot Line in the Mulhouse area.

Hitler welcomed Robert Wagner, Gauleiter of Baden-Elsass, to 'Tannenberg'. From left to right, Josef Bürckel, Gauleiter of Saar-Palatinate, Hans Lammers, head of the Reich Chancellery, Bormann and (hidden behind Bormann) von Schirach; in the background, Major Engel. Note the 'Blockhaus' and 'Arbeitsbaracke' signs. (ATB/USNA)

The same group, except Engel. Note that the bridge over the ditch had white markings painted on the sides to make it easier to spot at night. (ATB/USNA)

A deputation of women of the local Arbeitsgau (Work District) of the Reichsarbeitsdienst (RAD, Reich Labour Service) were invited to 'Tannenberg' to a tea party with the Führer. (ATB/USNA)

SS-Obersturmbannführer Brandt, a member of Hitler's inner circle, hosted another table. Trained in surgery, Brandt joined the Nazi party in 1932 and became Hitler's escort doctor in 1934. Appointed Commissioner of Sanitation and Health in 1942, he participated in euthanasia programs and human experimentation. On April 16, 1945, he was arrested by the Gestapo while taking his family to the American lines. He was given a summary trial and sentenced to death but Himmler and Speer intervened and Brandt was released on May 2. Three weeks later he was arrested by the British. Accused of involvement in human experimentation and other war crimes, Brandt was indicted in late 1946 along with 22 others during the Doctors' Trial at Nuremberg. He was convicted and sentenced to death, and he and six other defendants were executed by hanging on June 2, 1948. (ATB/USNA)

This elaborate L-shaped hut was probably one of the existing buildings of the Air Defence facility on which Anlage 'Tannenberg' was established. It is very unlikely that the 85 square metre wooden hut built by the Organisation Todt for the FHQu, the 'Arbeitsbaracke', would have wasted so much space on this large open terrace. (ATB/USNA)

After the Battle had this aerial photograph taken in 1977 of the former 'Tannenberg' site.

On July 2, Jodl and Warlimont presented Hitler with the outline plan for the invasion of Great Britain. This same day, Hitler edited Jodl's draft of the OKW's final report on the campaign in the West. On the 3rd and 4th, he worked on the speech which he would read at the Reichstag on July 16.

Hitler left 'Tannenberg' in the morning of July 5 and, after visiting soldiers hospitalised at Freudenstadt, he boarded his train 'Amerika' at Oppenau. The train steamed off at 1.00 p.m. and arrived at Anhalter Bahnhof in Berlin at 3.00 p.m. on July 6. On his way to the Reichskanzlei, huge crowds gave him an enthusiastic reception.

The Führer-Begleit-Bataillon was then transferred to FHQu 'Ziegenberg' in preparation for Operation 'Seelöwe', and a small Wachkommando stayed behind at 'Tannenberg' until the facility was taken over by the local military district later in 1940.

In early April 1945, units of US V Corps reached Anlage 'Tannenberg', which German engineers had blown up a few days earlier.

Remains were removed in 1946 and 1947, and the rubble served as building material for the population for years. What was left was finally removed in the early 1960s and the foundations of the buildings levelled.

FHQU 'WALDWIESE'

FHQu 'Waldwiese', established at Glan-Münchweiler, 25 kilometres west of Kaiserslautern, was the only one of four FHQu built on the Western Front from October 1939 to May 1940 never to have been used. Therefore, although FHQu 'Waldwiese' appears as the second in the list of these four in the Schmelcher report, we chose to study it last.

On the afternoon of June 28, Hitler left FHQu 'Tannenberg' in an automobile column to visit Strasbourg and meet General Friedrich Dollmann, commander of the 7. Armee. Keitel and Bormann were part of the trip. Two days later the party returned to Alsace to inspect casemates of the Maginot Line.

Hitler left FHQu 'Tanneberg' in the morning of July 5 and then visited soldiers in a military hospital Freudenstadt. He boarded his train at Oppenau in the afternoon and he was back to Berlin at 3.00 p.m. on the 6th.

Work began in early October, construction required 38,750 working days and 4,250 cubic metres of concrete. The maximum workforce on site was 500 people in December. Completed in April 1940 the work provided 285 square metres of usable space in three bunkers, and 96 in two wooden huts. The Führerbunker was on the wooded hill just east of Glan-Münchweiler and the communications bunker was in the centre of the village. It was disguised as a dwelling house with a slate roof and painted windows on the walls. The third bunker was on the hill southwest of the village. In addition, the Organisation Todt reported road construction and camouflage work.

Schmelcher's report points that these constructions were only for a small part of the FHQu itself, nothing being built to house the services of the OKH or the Reichsführer-SS.

Hitler never used 'Waldwiese' and we could not find out what the complex was used for during the war. Units of the US 76th Infantry Division reached 'Anlage Waldwiese' in early April 1945 and found it intact. American engineers blew up two bunkers in the summer of 1946 and the concrete rubble was recycled by the locals in the post-war years. In the village, the communications bunker was only demolished in the early 1960s. Today, only a few nondescript pieces of concrete remain in the woods.

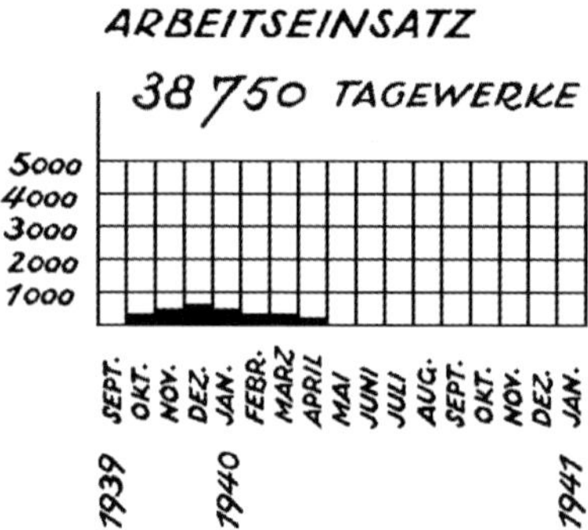

STOLLEN | MASSIVHÄUSER UND UMMANTELTE BARACK | BUNKER UND STOLLEN EINGANGE | BARACKEN, BLOCK HÄUSER UND FACH-WERKSHÄUSER | MASS…

BETON… DER BU… MASSIVH… UND DER… MANTE… BARAC…

ZUSAMMENSTELLUNG

285 m2 | 96 m2 | 425…

This sketch from the Schmelcher's report indicates that construction of FHQu 'Waldwiese' from October 1939 through April 1940 involved a total of 38,750 working days and needed 4,250 cubic metres of concrete. Quite modest figures compared to those observed at the FHQu 'Ziegenberg' or the FHQu 'Felsennest'.

According to this report, the works provided 285 square metres of useful space in heavy bunkers and 96 square metres in wooden huts or blockhouse.

In the woods just east of Glan-Münchweiler, Michelle Pfeiffer took this photo of what may be the remains of the Führerbunker. (Michelle Pfeiffer, The Rheinpfalz)

'Access to the steps is prohibited!' This warning inscription on a stone step in front of the remains of the bunker is the most remarkable witness to the otherwise completely erased site. (Michelle Pfeiffer, The Rheinpfalz)

It is reported that this bunker located on the hill southwest of Glan-Münchweiler also belonged to the FHQu complex. (Michelle Pfeiffer, The Rheinpfalz)

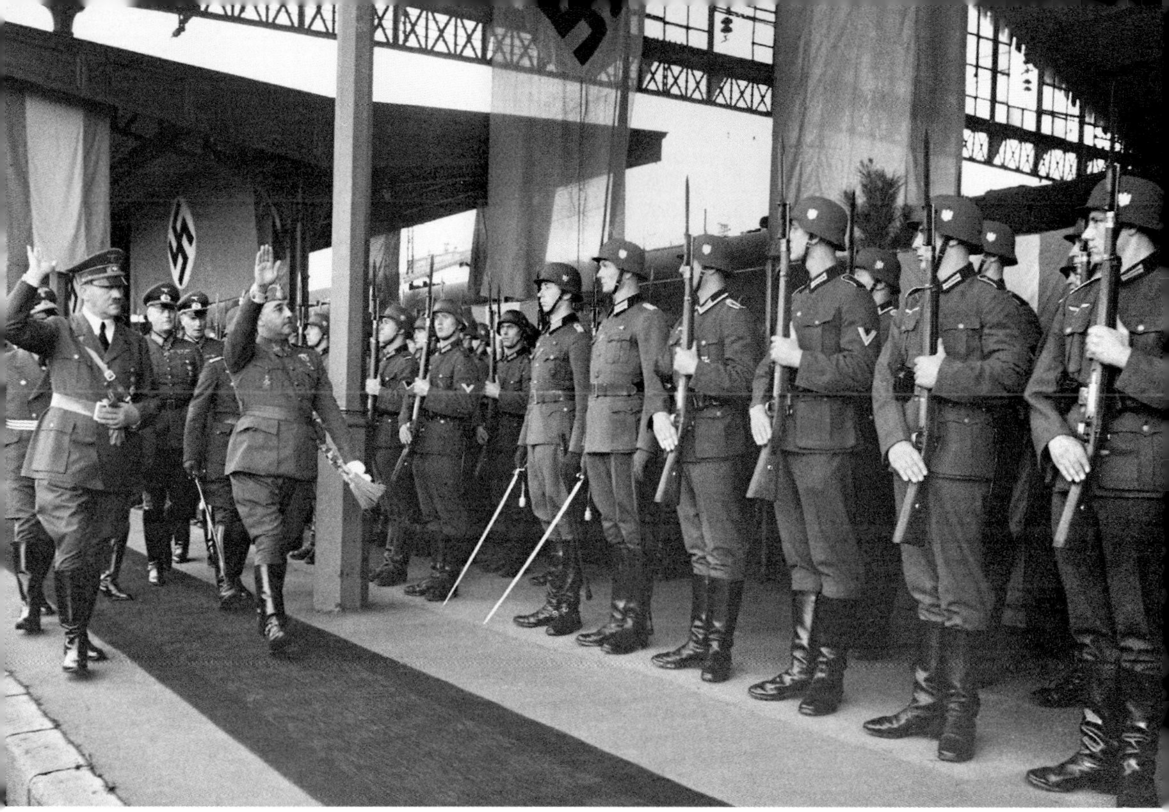

In October 1940, Hitler used the Führersonderzug, his special train, to travel to France where he held three diplomatic meetings, one with Pierre Laval to prepare the meeting with Maréchal Pétain, then with Francisco Franco in Hendaye, near the Spanish border (the trains could not go longer as the width of the Spanish rails was larger than the standard ones at the time), and then with Maréchal Pétain in Montoire-sur-le-Loir, a small French town 200 kilometres south-west from Paris. The Hendaye railway station, Then and Now.

THE CAMPAIGN IN THE BALKANS, 1941, FHQU 'FRÜHLINGSSTURM'

AFTER THE POLISH CAMPAIGN, Hitler often used the Führersonderzug to travel from Berlin to Munich on his way to Berchtesgaden and Obersalzberg. In October 1940, he made his longest journey in the Führersonderzug to meet Francisco Franco, Spanish head of state, at Hendaye on the Spanish border, on the 23rd. On the way back, the train stopped at Montoire for a conference with the French head of state, Maréchal Pétain, on the 24th. The two conferences were unsuccessful since neither Franco nor Pétain could be convinced to enter the war against Great Britain. Having learned that Mussolini planned to invade Greece, Hitler ordered the Führersonderzug to rush to Florence for a meeting with Mussolini on the 28th, in an attempt to stop the Italian enterprise. Three hours before arriving at Florence, the Germans received confirmation that the Italian attack had begun.

At Christmas 1940, Hitler travelled to France with the Führersonderzug to visit Wehrmacht units. The train spent the night of the 22nd in a tunnel near Boulogne and the next day Hitler visited long-range artillery batteries and teams of the Organisation Todt. The train stood in a tunnel near Beauvais on the nights of the 24th and 25th and Hitler visited Luftwaffe units, having lunch on Christmas Day with a bomber squadron.

From April 12 to April 27, 1941, the Führersonderzug again served as Führerhauptquartier during the Balkan campaign. Code named FHQu 'Frühlingssturm', the train was parked in the small mountain station of Mönichkirchen, Austria, 70 kilometres southwest of Vienna. A few hundred metres to the south was the northern entrance to the Great Hartberg tunnel that could offer suitable shelter for the train.

Work in the tunnel served as a pretext for the evacuation of the station and the hotel Mönichkirchnerhof nearby and in two weeks 500 men from the Organisation Todt developed the necessary infrastructure: additional tracks, platform to facilitate boarding and alighting (this was only for Hitler's saloon car, wooden stairs being prepared for other cars), sewers and radio connections.

The Führer-Begleit-Bataillon secured the surrounding area with some 1,150 men, with quarters in Mönichkirchen and Aspang.

The Führersonderzug 'Amerika' arrived in Mönichkirchen, Austria, at 7.20 a.m. on April 12, 1941. Parked in the small mountain station there until April 26, the train served as the Führerhauptquartier 'Frühlingssturm' during the campaign in the Balkans. The train's two Flakwagens, here coupled together, with Hotel Mönichkirchnerhof in mid distance. (ATB/USNA)

The new Sonderzug 'Atlas' of the Wehrmachtführungsstab arrived on the evening of April 11 and was parked in the southern part of the Hartberg tunnel. The Führersonderzug arrived in Mönichkirchen at 7.20 a.m. on April 12, two hours later than scheduled, as light snow was falling. A handcar ensured the fast connection between the two trains through the tunnel.

Göring's Sonderzug 'Asien' parked in the Wiesenhöfe Tunnel north of Friedberg, a few kilometres south of Hitler's location, Himmler's Sonderzug 'Heinrich' parked at Brück an der Mur, west of Mönichkirchen, and von Ribbentrop's Sonderzug 'Westfalen' parked in Vienna's Südbahnhof. The OKH used the Maria Theresa Academy facilities in Wiener-Neustadt.

Except for short walks to the Mönichkirchnerhof, where he watched the latest newsreels, Hitler did not venture from his Sonderzug beyond the station platform.

On April 19, he received King Boris III of Bulgaria. On April 20, he celebrated his 52nd birthday, and well-wishers included Franz von Papen, then German Ambassador to Turkey, Generaloberst von Brauchitsch, Admiral Erich Raeder, and Italian Foreign Minister Gian Galeazzo Ciano.

This is the north end of the train, the locomotives are just out of sight to the right. In 1977, Winston Ramsey, the then Editor of *After the Battle*, found the small Mönichkirchen station unchanged since Hitler's day except that the wooden platform and siding have been removed. The same curve of the rail track in September 1977. (ATB/USNA)

On April 24, the Hungarian regent, Admiral Miklos Horthy, visited Hitler to secure Hungary a territorial share in the partition of Yugoslavia.

With Yugoslavia having signed an armistice on April 17, the leaders of the German attack reached Athens, the capital of Greece, on April 27.

At 2 a.m. on April 26, with the campaign soon to end with a victory, the Führersonderzug left Mönichkirchen for southern Austria so that Hitler could visit Graz and Marburg. He slept on board the train during the night and, after visiting Klagenfurt on the 27th, he returned to his train which departed in the evening. He returned to Berlin at 6.30 p.m. on April 28.

The two locomotives would push the train into the Great Hartberg tunnel in the event of an attack by enemy aircraft. Looking southwards, with Hotel Mönichkirchnerhof in mid distance.

The Führersonderzug 'Amerika' standing on the single-line track, looking north. This is the south end of the train and a few hundred metres in the back of the photographer was the entrance to the Great Hartberg tunnel. (ATB/USNA)

On the morning of April 13, Generaloberst von Brauchitsch, Army C-in-C, arrived from Wiener-Neustadt to attend a conference. (ATB/USNA)

Hitler, war leader. The scene was perfect for propaganda and more than a dozen photos were taken of Hitler discussing the situation in the Balkans with Generals von Brauchitsch and Keitel in the Führersonderzug. (ATB/USNA)

Another photo taken in the first days of the stay at Mönichkirchen, when SS-Gruppenführer Julius Schaub, Hitler's new chief adjutant, led Göring to the Befehlswagen (command car). Göring's train was parked in the Wiesenhöfe tunnel, a few kilometres south of Mönichkirchen. (ATB/USNA)

During his stay at the station, Hitler did not venture beyond the station platform, except for short walks to a small hotel near the station, the Mönichkirchnerhof, where he viewed the latest newsreels. (ATB/USNA)

Julius Schaub, Hitler, and Walther Hewel, von Ribbentrop's liaison officer, walk along the platform built by the Organisation Todt to facilitate boarding and alighting the train. NSKK-Brigadeführer Albert Bormann, Martin Bormann's younger brother, is behind Schaub. The same curve of the rail track in September 1977. Trains no longer stopped at all at Mönichkirchen, with the local station now at Aspang only a few kilometres away. (ATB/USNA)

On April 15, Hitler leaves Hotel Mönichkirchnerhof with Bormann on his right and Schaub at his left. The hotel owners were then Ferdinand and Emma Awart. In 1977, Winston Ramsey found the Mönichkirchnerhof still in business. The hotel closed in the 1990s but the building still exists. (ATB/USNA)

Hitler enters the Bahnhof forecourt after leaving the hotel. The tall Luftwaffe officer (second from left with movie camera) is Walter Frentz. (ATB/USNA)

On April 15, officers are introduced to Hitler on the road outside the Hotel Mönichkirchnerhof. It appears that most of them were Luftwaffe officers and this presentation may have been made when the Flak unit assigned to the anti-aircraft defense of the FHQu was reinforced and reorganised, increasing from five to eight batteries. The unit then took the name of I. Abteilung, Flak-Regiment 604. (ATB/USNA)

Mönichkirchen, a scene that had changed little in 1977 when *After the Battle* was here.

Returning from the hotel, Hitler and Schaub passed the station (on the right of the photo) and walked along the platform towards the Führerwagen. Winston Ramsey had just a minute to take this comparison photo in 1977, before catching the train to Vienna before it leaves. This was the head of the diesel-powered train. (ATB/USNA)

Scenes of daily life at the FHQu 'Frühlingssturm'. An SS-Hauptsturmführer of the Führer-Begleit-Kommando ensures that his men's boots are clean, and operators at work at the train's telephone exchange in the Befehlswagen. Note the 'Adolf Hitler' cuff title worn by the SS-Untersturmführer on the right. (ATB/USNA)

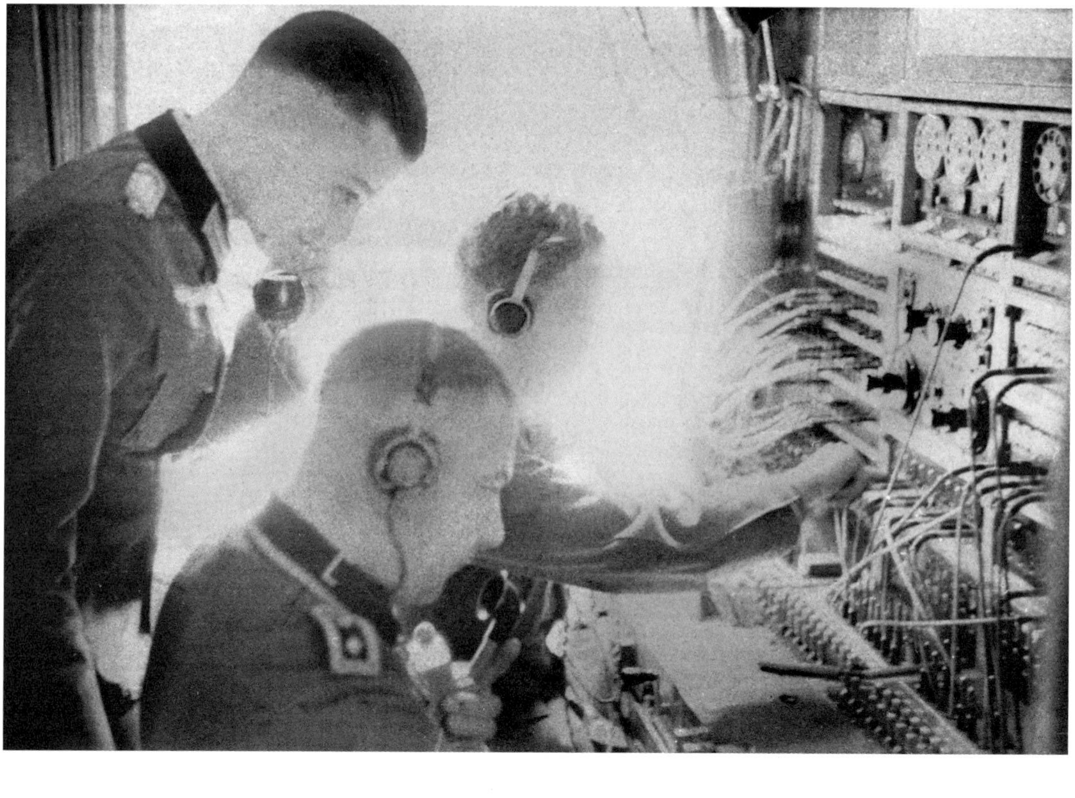

On April 19, Hitler received King Boris III of Bulgaria. Officials waited his arrival on the platform. In dark uniform, Franz von Papen, Ambassador to Turkey, in the centre, Walther Hewell, von Ribbentrop's liaison officer with Hitler. (ATB/USNA)

Von Ribbentrop greeted the Bulgarian delegation. (ATB/USNA)

King Boris then arrived, in civilian clothes, and von Ribbentrop led him along the platform to meet Hitler in front of the Führerwagen. On the left is Schaub and on the right Gustav Steengracht von Moyland, an assistant of von Ribbentrop. This car, SalBer4ü-38a, number 10 252 Bln, was the conference car. In post-war occupied Germany, it was used by the US Army before being returned to the German Railways in the early 1950s. (ATB/USNA)

Hitler celebrated his 52nd birthday at Mönichkirchen on April 20 and leaders of the Third Reich came to FHQu 'Frühlingssturm' to deliver their wishes personally. Reichsmarschall Göring is greeted on the platform by Keitel. Generalmajor Karl Bodenschatz, Göring's liaison officer with Hitler, looks on. (ATB/USNA)

Himmler, whose Sonderzug 'Heinrich' was parked at Brück an der Mur, also came to Mönichkirchen. Hitler, Himmler and Göring discussed on the platform. In the background was SS-Gruppenführer Otto Dietrich, Reich Press Chief. (ATB/USNA)

Among the well-wishers was Oberstleutnant Kurt Thomas, the FHQu commandant. (ATB/USNA)

The group then reviewed the troops sent to the FHQu to greet the Führer on his birthday. Mönichkirchen station was closed in 1996 and trains no longer stop at this remote place. Built in 1910, the abandoned building is now listed as a historic monument. On the other side of the railway tracks, the former station master's house is today occupied privately. (Priwo)

1941, 1942 AND 1943, OCCASIONAL STAYS AT BERGHOF

ON JUNE 24, 1941, two days after the begin of Operation 'Barbarossa', the attack against Soviet Union, the Führersonderzug arrived at the Forst Görlitz station and Hitler and his entourage took quarters to FHQu 'Wolfschanze'. For three years, the Führerhauptquartier remained at 'Wolfschanze', (with short stay at FHQu 'Askania Süd' in Poland and FHQu 'Wehrwolf' in Ukraine), by far the longest stay of the FHQu at any place over the course of the war.

Late in April 1942, Hitler met with Mussolini for a conference on Axis war strategy. Gian Galeazzo and Joachim von Ribbentrop, the Italian and German Foreign Ministers, arrived at the Berghof. (ATB/USNA)

Attending were Generalfeldmarschall Albert Kesselring, the Commander-in-Chief Süd, and Generale Ugo Cavallero, chief of Comando Supremo, the Italian High Command. After two days of conference, April 29 and 30, it was agreed that the invasion of Malta (codenamed Operation 'Hercules') would take place in mid-July, with an airborne assault with a German airborne division and an Italian airborne division, followed by a seaborne landing of two or three divisions. (ATB/USNA)

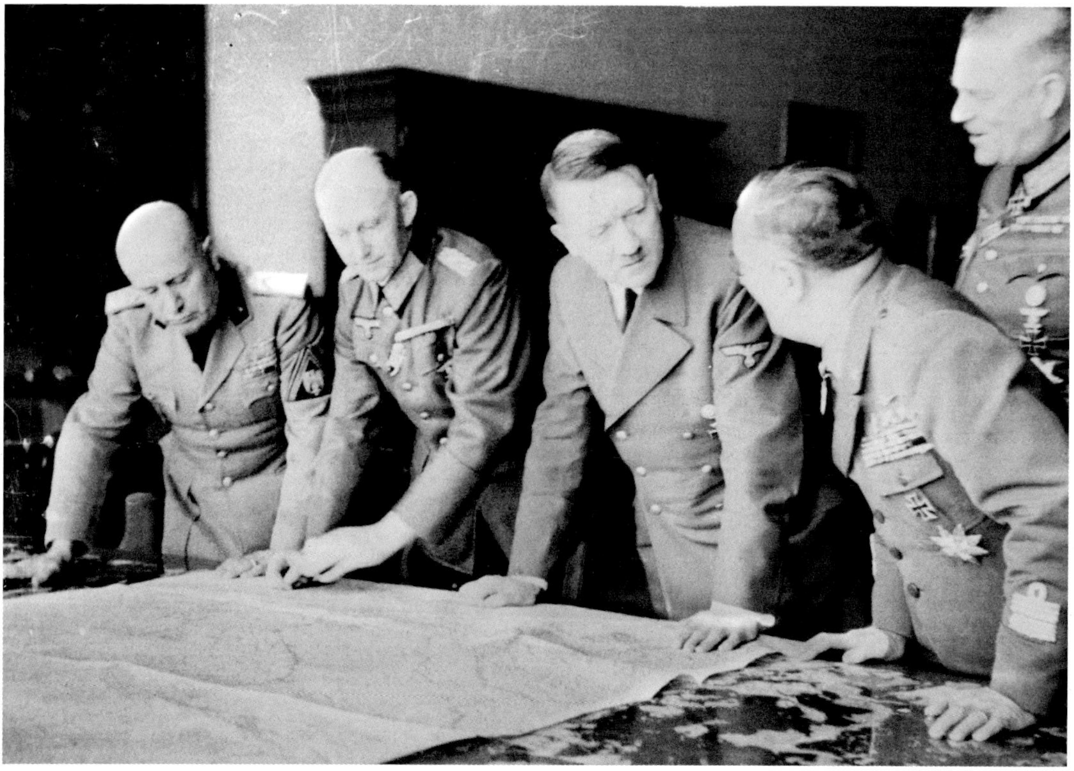

The Great Room of the Berghof served as a reception and conference room. This view shows the left-rear corner of the room and the west wall. The doorway in the right background led into the living area of the building. (ATB/USNA)

Hitler only stayed at the Berghof for a few days in April and June 1942 and ten days in November.

In 1943, Hitler stayed at the Berghof for a month from late March, and on the 31st he received King Boris III of Bulgaria to urge him to implement the deportation of the Jews from his kingdom, and join the war against the Soviet Union. From April 7, he conferred for three days with Mussolini at the Klessheim Castle, near Salzburg, but the conference served only to increase the growing friction between the Third Reich and Italy.

On April 20, Hitler celebrated his 54th birthday at the Berghof, and on the 29th he received French Prime Minister Pierre Laval and Italian Undersecretary at the Foreign Ministry Giuseppe Bastianini.

He returned to his eastern FHQu at the end of June and remained there until the end of February 1944, except for a one-week stay at the Berghof in November 1943. He returned to the Berghof on February 24 and remained there for four and a half months, with a day trip to 'Wolfsschlucht 2' on June 17, and a day trip to 'Wolfschanze' on July 9. It was his last stay at the Berghof.

He left on July 15 and arrived on the 16th at FHQu 'Wolfschanze'. Four days later, Oberst Claus von Stauffenberg attempted to kill him by detonating a bomb in the conference room.

As nothing remains of the Berghof, it is impossible to take comparison photos. However, this photo taken in 1945 by Thérèse Bonney offers a remarkable comparison with a photo taken when Mussolini was leaving the Berghof. This five-window circular extension was the coffee corner of the dining room in the eastern wing. (Thérèse Bonney, The Bancroft Library, University of California, Berkeley, and ATB/USNA)

Hitler, followed by Keitel and Brückner, led his guest down the stairs to his car which was parked in the driveway.
(ATB/USNA)

In 1943, Hitler stayed at the Berghof from March 22 to May 2, and from May 21 to June 30, and he stayed for a week in November. On March 31, Hitler received King Boris III to urge him to initiate the deportation of Jews from Bulgaria and join the war against the Soviet Union. Discussion in the great hall of the Berghof, King Boris, von Ribbentrop and Hitler. (USNA)

Unlike the Kehlsteinhaus where he rarely went, Hitler went almost every afternoon to the Mooslahnerkopf teahouse, a 20-minute walk. This photo was taken on April 14, 1943. American authorities demolished the building in the 1950s to prevent it from becoming a pilgrimage site for neo-Nazis and the remains were finally removed in 2006. The panoramic view point still exists. (USNA)

On April 20, Hitler celebrated his 54th birthday at the Berghof. He looks here at the photos in a souvenir album that Hoffmann has just offered him, on the right Baldur von Schirach. In the background, Herta Schneider, a friend of Eva Braun from childhood, Christa Schroeder, one of Hitler's personal secretaries, and Karl Brandt. (USNA)

On the 29th Hitler received French Prime Minister Pierre Laval and Italian Undersecretary at the Foreign Ministry Giuseppe Bastianini. (USNA)

FÜHRERHAUPTQUARTIER 'WOLFSSCHLUCHT 2'

IN MARCH 1942, as an invasion attempt by the Allies was expected at some stage, Hitler issued his Directive No. 40 for the conduct of the defence of the West. He decreed that the defences along the coast should be organised in such a way that any invasion attempt could be smashed before the actual landing or certainly immediately after. In the spring, the building of the 'Atlantic Wall' began. At the same time, it was decided to establish a battle headquarters in France from where Hitler could conduct operations personally when the expected invasion by the Western Allies took place.

Although it is not clear when the decision to establish this advanced HQ was precisely reached, the first mention of 'Anlage W 2' appears in the FHQu war diary in June 1942. In May, Oberst Thomas and Major Walter Spengemann flew from FHQu 'Wolfschanze' in East Prussia, where Hitler and his entourage were then in residence, to Brussels and Paris to discuss the setting up of the new Führerhauptquartier and to reconnoitre possible sites. In the end they settled on Margival as, just north of the village, the tunnel that was necessary to provide shelter for the Führersonderzug had now been repaired. Although Hitler had seen action in this sector in May 1918 when he was a soldier with the Bayerische Reserve-Infanterie-Regiment 16, it is doubtful that he chose the Margival site himself.

In September 1942, the director of the OT, Xaver Dorsch, ordered Hauptbauleiter Schmelcher to start construction of 'Wolfsschlucht 2'. (Dr Todt had been appointed Minister for Armaments and Munitions in March 1940; by then, Xaver Dorsch had taken over as head of the Organisation Todt.)

To manage the construction of the new Führerhauptquartier a local command of the OT – Oberbauleitung 'Wolfsschlucht 2' – was set up at Soissons under Bauassessor Friedrich Classen.

Construction work began in September and from then on, the railway tunnel was closed to normal traffic. Ventilation shafts were installed with smoke extractors providing a fresh air supply even when locomotives under steam were parked inside. Two sets of armoured doors were fitted, one 80 metres from the exit at Margival while the other was 120 metres inside the Vauxaillon entrance. Each door was made of two sections which slid into recesses cut into the sides of the tunnel. The small railway station at the southern end, which had been established in 1921 to serve the villages of Laffaux and Neuville-sur-Margival, was enlarged and the existing platform lengthened. On October 25, 1942, Oberst Engel came with Hauptbauleiter

Tak… his photo shows that the Teehaus (tea house), the… dings to be erected in the compound and that con… üller)

The… the Führersonderzüg (Hitler's special train), disa… ed, but two of the buildings constructed later – Ba…

This beautiful photo of Bau 1, the Führerbunker, with the Teehaus on the hillside in the background, was taken in the 1980s by Pierre Rhode and Werner Sünkel. In 1993 they published *Wolfsschlucht 2, Autopsie eines Führerhauptquartiers*, a remarkably detailed study of the Margival headquarters. (P. Rhode and W. Sünkel)

Schmelcher and his deputy, Oberbauleiter Leo Müller, to visit Classen and discuss the expansion of 'Wolfsschlucht 2', abbreviated 'W 2'. On December 17 Engel returned a second time to give Müller further instructions.

The construction of 'Wolfsschlucht 2' was a masterpiece of logistics. Because local material was unsuitable for making concrete, sand, ballast, and cement had to be imported, mainly by barge from Belgium, being unloaded at Missy-sur-Aisne, about eight kilometres away. Other materials like iron and timber arrived by rail at Crouy station, between Margival and Soissons.

As 'W 2' lay in a remote rural area, the telephone network had to be extended from Paris to reach it using some 115 kilometres of cabling. From the French capital there were two trunk lines to Germany, one to Aachen via Brussels, the other to Saarbrücken through Reims and Metz. A further trunk line via Charleville was also extended through Belgium to Prüm in Germany so the HQ would have a third point of access to the Reich network.

Electricity was provided from the French civilian grid by underground

In September 1944, an investigation team from the US 602nd Engineer Camouflage Battalion surveyed the 'Wolfsschlucht 2' compound and took this picture of the camouflaged Bau 1 which blended remarkably well with the tree-lined slope behind. This photo clearly shows the wooden platform built for the Führersonderzüg. (USNA)

This photo was taken in September 1944, a few days after the last Germans had left, by the team from the 602nd Engineer Camouflage Battalion, show 'Wolfsschlucht 2' as it appeared under German occupancy. This picture illustrates well the words of Lieutenant Colonel Robert E. Kearney in his report to the US First Army: 'The camouflage measures taken throughout this area were excellent'. (USNA)

cables. To avoid the possibility of power cuts, emergency diesel generators housed in three separate concrete shelters were installed. Water was pumped in from springs in the surrounding hills and piped from there into a 500-cubic-metre reservoir. Three sewage farms were provided for dealing with waste water.

As virtually no photos of the 'Wolfschlucht 2' from the time of its use by the Germans appear to have survived, this series of photos taken during the first months of 1944 by Obergefreiter Schillings is of great interest. It seems that a delegation from the Stabs-Nachrichten-Kompanie (Signal Company) of FHQu 'Wolfschanze' then came to Margival to visit FHQu 'Wolfschlucht 2' (note the camouflaged bunker in the background). According to a surviving original caption, the team comprised Oberleutnant Radolff, Oberleutnant von Brockdorff, Fw. Ilger, Uffz. Maul, Uffz. Geidtner, Uffz. Scharnitzky, Uffz. Binder, Obgefr. Marx, Obgefr. Lüdecke, Obgefr. Haarmann, Obgefr. Conrad, Obgefr. von Stietenkron, Obgefr. Matting, Gefr. Guthausen and Sonderführer Schorath.

Oberleutnant Radolff, Oberleutnant von Brockdorff (of the Luftwaffe) and Feldwebel Ilger posed with their Citroën car for a souvenir photo for the family album. Vregny château, Then and Now.

On the porch in front of the château, Oberleutnant Radolff and Oberleutnant von Brockdorff posed with Bauassessor Friedrich Classen, the Oberbauleiter responsible for the construction of 'Wolfschlucht 2'. Rank and functions are often misleading for the Organisation Todt managers because their functional assignment (e.g. Oberbauleiter) can be confused with their rank in the civil servant hierarchy (e.g. Baussessor). As shown by the national police emblem visible on his cap and left sleeve, the man on the right was a member of a police unit.

In December 1942 the work-force comprised 7,000 men but this was progressively increased to 10,000 by February 1943, 12,000 by March, reaching a peak of 13,000 in April. It then decreased to 4,000 in July to reach 3,000 for the remainder of the year. Much of the labour was provided by French building firms contracted to the Organisation Todt but in addition French, Belgian, Dutch, and later Italian, prisoners of war and forced labour were also employed. While the OT employees were quartered either in the Charpentier Barracks in Soissons, commuting by train to Margival, or in huts, the impressed workers were housed in camps set up close to the building site. Bauassessor Classen and his engineers had established their offices and quarters in Le Moulin, just west of the village.

On March 20, 1943, Müller and Classen met with Oberst Engel and Oberstleutnant Gustav Streve, the new Führerhauptquartier Commander, in Berlin to consider progress, Müller seeing Engel again on April 4, this time at Obersalzberg, to discuss outstanding matters. On the 22nd, Müller and

Oberleutnant von Brockdorff and officers, presumably from the staff of FHQu 'W 2', observed men setting up a radio station on the hill overlooking Bau 2 (see aerial view page 116). Note the two antennas planted in the ground.

Still with Oberleutnant von Brockdorff in the middle, the team posed in front of Bau 2, the OKW bunker. One of seven 'Baustärke A' heavy bunkers of FHQu 'W 2', this bunker had a 'Vorbau' annex along its front and sides plus an independent building located at the front right-hand corner.

Oberleutnant Radolff and Oberleutnant von Brockdorff (left) with some of their men in front of Bau 15, one of the 13 light bunkers in the inner compound of 'W 2'. The size of the trees very close to the bunker proves that the Germans had transplanted already large trees to replant them around the new constructions, and thus camouflage them.

With a length of over 100 metres, Bau 5 is the largest of the constructions at 'W 2'. The 'Vorbau' (annex) along its front masks the 'Baustärke A' (build-strength A) heavy bunker lying behind. In the right background is Bau 6 of lighter construction.

Then and Now. Another photo of the same series, of signal men at work in the telephone exchange. Rooms in the 'Vorbau' annex (above) and inside the main 'Baustärke A' bunker (right).

There were seven heavy bunkers of 'Baustärke A' in the inner compound. This photo taken in 1982, during French use of the site, shows a well-maintained Bau 4, a bunker of the 'Baustärke A' type, that during the war had housed the FHQu teleprinter exchange. In the background, across the railway line, stands Bau 1. The original German concrete road was still in perfect condition. (Michel Truttmann)

Depending on their size, the bunkers of 'Baustärke A' comprised either one or several separate shelters, with a gas-lock at each entrance. Bau 1 and 4 comprised only one shelter, Bau 2, 21 and 23 (this plan here) two, Bau 9 three and Bau 5 four. Most of these bunkers had an annex, or 'Vorbau', comprising overflow offices with walls and ceilings only 50 to 75cm thick.

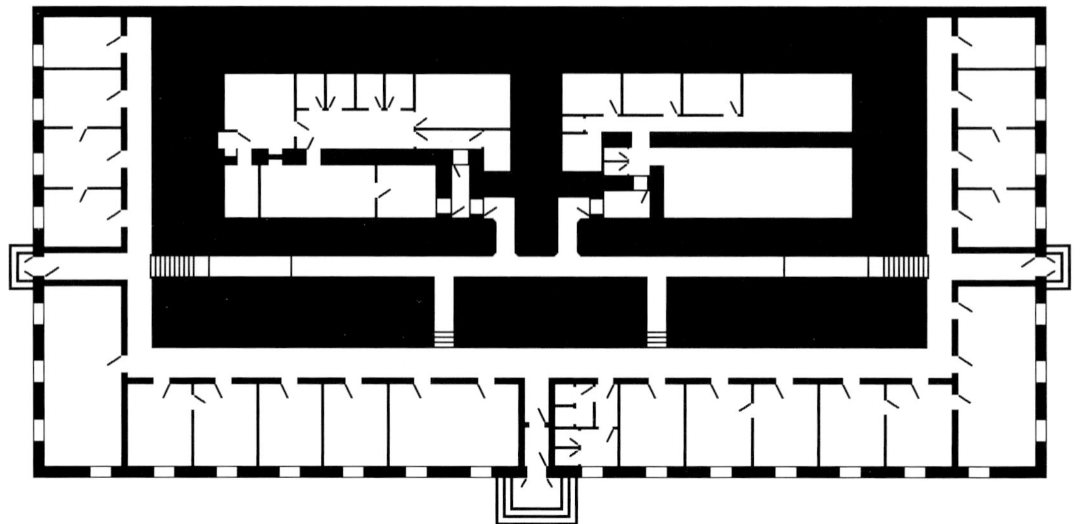

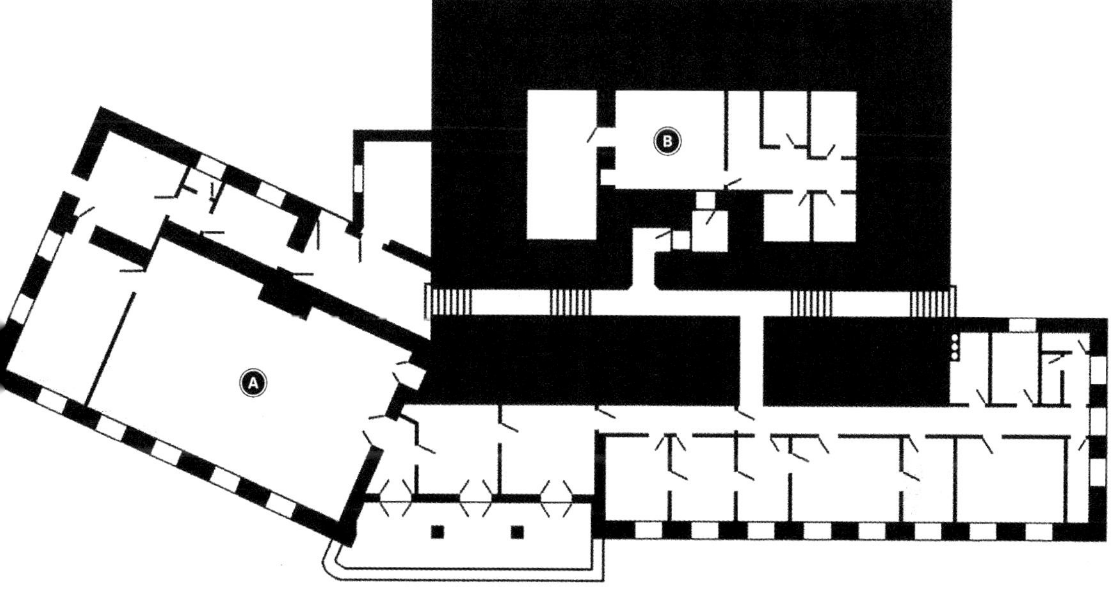

Some of these extensions were shaped to make the best use of the hillside on which they were built, hence the angled Bau 1 (this plan here) and the curved Bau 5. This was the Führerbunker where the meeting of June 17 took place. It began at 9.30 a.m. in the conference room in the 'Vorbau' [A] and lasted till 12.30 p.m. when lunch was served in the nearby Teehaus. The talks resumed in the afternoon, but were interrupted by an air raid warning, which sent Hitler and the two field-marshals to the shelter in the heavy bunker [B]. They remained there for about an hour, finally emerging about 3 p.m., and von Rundstedt and Rommel left soon thereafter.

Classen had a site meeting to discuss electrification and camouflage and on May 27 Müller flew over the site in a Fieseler Storch to check the latter from the air. In November, when an impending inspection by Oberstleutnant von Below was announced, Müller called on his supervisors to urge them to step up the pace. Then, before returning to Munich, Müller called at the Paris office to confer with Oberbaudirektor Weiss, the head of OT Einsatzgruppe West (Assignment Group West), which was the OT operational command covering France, Belgium, Holland, and the Channel Islands. Müller made his last visit to Margival on January 10, 1944, to inspect the air conditioning system. By then, the construction of Führerhauptquartier 'Wolfsschlucht 2' was nearly complete.

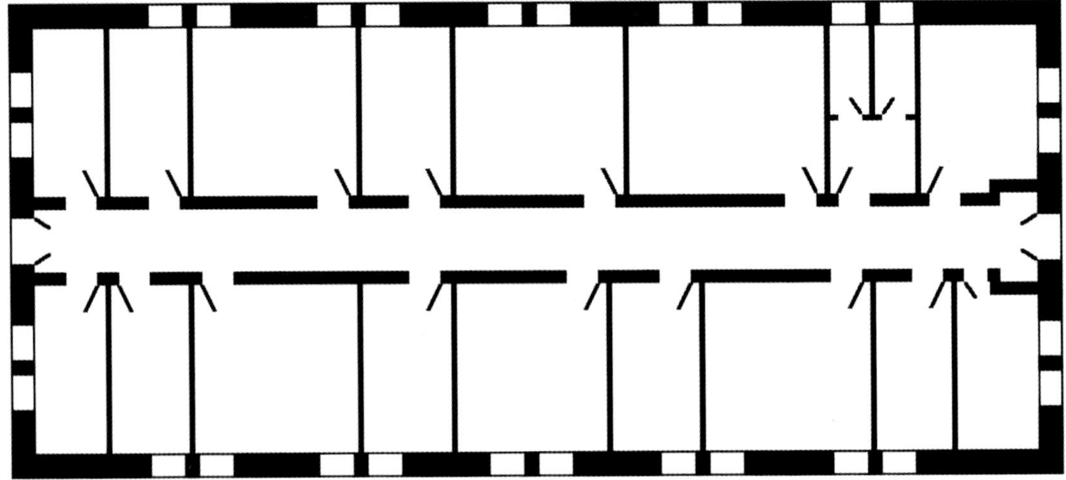

There were 13 light bunkers in the inner compound. Bau 15, shown here, illustrates the general plan of these bunkers, which had a central corridor with entrances at each end and offices on either side. Depending on its size, each bunker featured between ten and 20 rooms plus a toilet.

During the 1970s, the French Army gave the large bunkers girl's names which were painted on the concrete. Bau 1 became 'Marie-Aude', Bau 2 'Marie-Jeanne', Bau 5 'Constance', and so on. In the early 1980s, the bunkers were renamed along more-martial lines, Bau 1 becoming 'Haut-le-Wastia' after the battle with the Germans in Belgium in May 1940. Others commemorated Napoléon's campaign in Italy in 1795, like Bau 9, 'Zucarello', and Bau 21, 'Loano', or his Russian campaign, with the name 'Bérézina', the memorable river crossing in November 1812. Others commemorated battles of the First World War such as 'La Marne' and 'Verdun'. This corner of Bau 10 still shows the successive designations of the bunker. The first series of numbers, here number '10', which probably followed the original German numbering system, was painted directly on the concrete in white on a black background. The girls' names were also painted directly on the concrete, and we see in this photo the blue outline of this name protruding slightly from the metal panels bearing the new name, 'Sergent Coty'. These were painted in red on blue metal panels which were secured to the concrete. The same method of adding metal panels was used for the new three-digit numbers, here '037'.

Bau 6 and Bau 7 were two of the light bunkers. 'Derly' in the French naming of the bunkers in the 1980s, the former measures 29.4 by 11.4 metres; the latter, 'A/C Bahl', mesures 34 by 12 metres.

Numerous Flak batteries and a belt of ground defences protected the headquarters out as far as Vauxaillon in the north to Chivres-Val to the south, a distance of some ten kilometres, and about four kilometres from Tergny-Sorny in the west to Laffaux in the east. The defence of the inner compound was the responsibility of the Führer-Begleit-Bataillon, which manned the control posts and sentry points on the perimeter.

In March 1944, the entire population of seven local villages – Laffaux,

The old installations for heating and ventilation still survive in Bau 5, the former telephone exchange. The presence of toxic materials, particularly asbestos (as can be seen here) forbids all visit in those rooms.

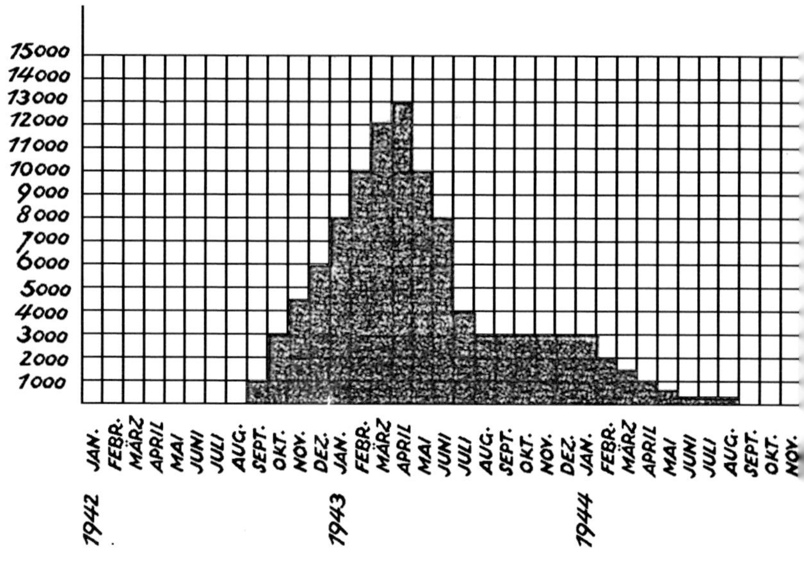

This sketch from Schmelcher's report filed in November 1944 describes the workforce engaged in the construction of the Führerhauptquartier at Margival from September 1942 through August 1944, a peak of 13,000 workers being reached in April 1944. The construction of 'Wolfsschlucht 2' involved a total of 2.7 million working days and needed 249,350 cubic metres of concrete. Concrete production by the Organisation Todt was incredibly large quantities for the time. The largest of the OT projects was the construction of the Atlantic Wall between August 1940 and June 1944, more than 10,000 fortifications and nearly 850 gun emplacements, which required 10.6 million cubic metres of concrete. The construction of the U-Boat bunkers consumed 4.4 million cubic metres, that for the Luftwaffe a million cubic metres and the various V-weapons storage and launch bunkers half a million cubic metres. The construction of the 19 FHQu listed in the Schmelcher report required nearly 1.1 million cubic metres of concrete.

STOLLEN
MASSIVHÄUSER UND UMMANTELTE BARACK
BUNKER UND STOLLEN EINGANGE
BARACKEN, BLOCK HÄUSER UND FACH-WERKSHÄUSER
MASSEN
BETONMENGE DER BUNKER, MASSIVHÄUSER UND DER UMMANTELTEN BARACKEN

STOLLEN	MASSIVHÄUSER UND UMMANTELTE BARACK	BUNKER UND STOLLEN EINGANGE	BARACKEN, BLOCK HÄUSER UND FACH-WERKSHÄUSER	MASSEN
1 mm - 2000 m²	1 mm - 2000 m²	1 mm - 2000 m²	1 mm - 2000 m²	1 mm - 2000 m³
ZUSAMMENSTELLUNG				
	15330	5045	22675	249350

According to this report, the constructions at Führerhauptquartier 'W 2' provided 43,050 square metres of useful space, of which 5,045 square metres were in heavy bunker of 'Baustärke A' standard. The figures on the left column are for tunnels dug out or fitted out by the OT, none in this case. The second column refers to the 'Ummantelte Baracken', concrete-encased huts that were only 'splittersicher' – shrapnel proof. The figures in the third column refer to heavy bunkers and the fourth to wooden huts, blockhouses, and other constructions. These four columns give figures in square metres. The column on the right gives, in cubic metres, the total amount of concrete used. The document reports that the constructions for 'Wolfsschlucht 2' were not only for the Führerhauptquartier, but also for the OKH, the RAM (Reichsaussenminister, Foreign Ministry) and the Reichsführer-SS. Nothing for the OKL. We only show the final page with the global figures here but another page details the construction for the FHQu and the OKH in the FHQu compound at Margival, and those that were done for Reichsführer-SS Heinrich Himmler and his staff at Vregny, five kilometres south of Margival, and for Foreign Minister Joachim von Ribbentrop and his staff at Mailly, 15 kilometres to the north-east.

Margival, Neuville-sur-Margival, Vauxaillon, Tergny-Sorny, Vregny and Vuillery – were evacuated, the German Wirtschaftsoberleitung (or WOL for short) taking over to run the farms in the area. Some minor defence work took place in the early summer when it was planned to incorporate the HQ into a defensive line across France.

No original plan of Führerhauptquartier 'W 2' appears to have survived and no photos of the headquarters during the war have been discovered. Although one can understand that the Germans would have banned all photography for security reasons, one might have hoped that the Americans or British would have photographed the base, assuming of course that they were aware of its importance as Hitler's headquarters in the West. However,

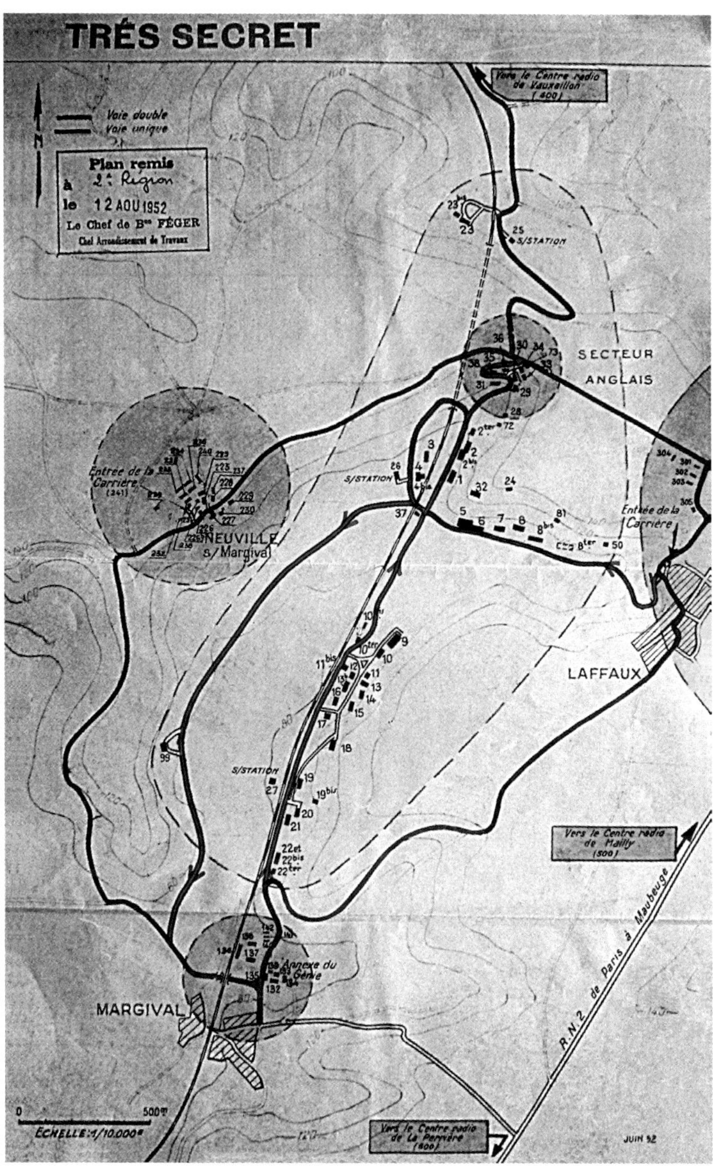

All in all, the Margival site comprised some 800 buildings, including 155 forming the ground defences and 230 the anti-aircraft batteries, plus another 80 miscellaneous structures serving as barracks, fuel stores, garages, etc. This plan, which is the earliest one of 'Wolfsschlucht 2' that we have been able to trace, was drawn up in June 1952 by French Army engineers when it was planned to use the former German headquarters for the French National Air Defence Command Centre. These plans index each construction from north to south with a two-digit reference number that may be based on the original German numbering, hence the description 'Bau 1' and 'Bau 2' that remained in use for the larger bunkers. More plans were drawn up in the 1970s and 1980s when the camp was occupied by the French Army but these changed the indexing to three figures. The yellow sector outlines the inner compound of 'W 2' but the buildings in the green areas were predominantly new French constructions except for those at Neuville-sur-Margival where there were original buildings from a German heavy Flak battery that had been located there. None of the wooden huts that were distributed throughout the area to serve as barracks for the Flak gun crews appear on this plan. These buildings were in poor shape by the early 1950s and by 1952 most of them had been demolished.

This arial photo was taken in April 1949 by the French Institut Géographique National (IGN) when Führerhauptquartier W 2 was still more or less as it was when the Germans vacated it in September 1944. The annotations accord with the French numbering of 1952. (IGN)

but for the survey conducted by the 602nd Engineer Camouflage Battalion in September 1944, no further investigation appears to have been carried out.

Führerhauptquartier 'W 2' covered an area two kilometres long by one wide and was split into two parts. The headquarters, with the Hitler and OKW bunkers and the communication centres, lay to the north while the support, supply and services were in the south. Surprisingly, there was no road inside

the compound linking the two parts until one was built in the 1950s along the eastern side of the railway line. According to Schmelcher's report, the constructions at Führerhauptquartier 'W 2' provided 43,050 square metres of useful space. Over ten per cent – 5,045 square metres – were built to what was called 'Baustärke A' standard, i.e. with walls and ceilings of 3.5 metres of reinforced concrete, capable of withstanding the heaviest artillery of the

FÜHRERHAUPTQUARTIER 'WOLFSSCHLUCHT 2' INNER COMPOUND

French indexing 1950s	*French indexing 1980s*	*Description*	*Overall measurements*		*FHQu function when known*	*Comments and later French names*
1	027	heavy bunker	23	17	Führerbunker	Haut le Wastia
		Vorbau	50	23		
2	002	heavy bunker	60	18.5	OKW	Zucarello
		Vorbau	72.5	25.5		
		annex	44	12		
4	028	heavy bunker	31	18.5	teleprinter exchange	
		Vorbau	11	20		
5	024	heavy bunker	93	18.5	telephone exchange	Constance
		Vorbau	108.5	25.5		
9	036	heavy bunker	69	18.5	guests' bunker	Taschet des Combes
		Vorbau	79.5	26		
21	056	heavy bunker	44.5	18.5	shelter	Loano
		annex	16	12	garage	
23	Vx 971	heavy bunker	45	18.5		
		Vorbau	60	26		
3	029	light bunker	27.4	13	cinema	Krasnoe
6	023	light bunker	29.4	11.4		Derly
7	022	light bunker	34	12		A/C Bahl
8	019	light bunker	29.4	11.4		Berezina
10	037	light bunker	32	14		Sergent Coty
13	046	light bunker	23	14		Verdun
14	047	light bunker	45	14		Fockedey
15	048	light bunker	32	14		Col Marescot du Tilleul
16	049	light bunker	44	14		La Marne
18	051	light bunker	35	14		Gal Weiller
19	052	light bunker	40	12.4		Caen
20	054	light bunker	32	14		SLt Busin
22	057	light bunker	40	12.4		Le Matz
26	030	power station	28.8	11	four 150 KVA generators	
27	060	power station	13.6	10.4	two 150 KVA generators	
25	Vx 970	power station	13.6	10.4	two 150 KVA generators	
17	050	shelter	16.7	15.5	Type 608	
11	039	shelter	14.8	9.5	Type 502	
12	044	shelter	12.5	11.6	Type 622	
19b	053	shelter	12.5	11.6	Type 622	
72	004	shelter	9.8	9.6	Type 621	
50	016	shelter	9.8	9.6	Type 621	
23b	Vx 467b	shelter	9.8	9.6	Type 621	
10b	040	wooden building	30.5	12.5		demolished 1970s
11b	043	wooden chalet	13	11		demolished 1980s
32	026	wooden chalet	26.5	6.4	officers club ('Teehaus')	demolished 1986
22t	058	brick building			entrance post	pre WWII construction
37	032	brick building			railway station	pre WWII construction

This table only lists the larger bunkers and specific constructions in the inner compound of 'Wolfsschlucht 2'. It does not include Flak or ground-defence bunkers. The first line for the heavy bunkers refers to the 'Baustärke A' part and the second to the annex or 'Vorbau'. These extensions were generally built along the front and sides of the central bunker and the measurements given include the annex, hence the latter line should be read as 'overall measurements' (except for Bau 4 and 21 where the annex was simply built alongside). The functions of each construction in the FHQu organisation remain largely unknown though in a very few cases some indications can be found in early reports. In the case of Bau 3 for example, the American engineers visiting the camp in September 1944 noted that it was a 'motion picture auditorium'.

day and direct hits from bombs of up to one tonne. These bunkers had their own air supply and could be sealed off from the outside, the entrances being protected by a pair of gas-proof armoured doors. These bunkers were not just air raid shelters but served to provide secure accommodation for command and communications (one of them housed the telephone exchange and another the teleprinter unit). The headquarters compound contained seven

Little is known about the entertainment facilities provided for the FHQu staff. There was a swimming pool (021) near the Teehaus (032) and it was used by the French in 1977 when *After the Battle* took this photograph. In *Wolfsschlucht 2, Autopsie eines Führerhauptquartiers* P. Rhode and W. Sünkel assumed that the 200 cubic metres of water was also intended for fire extinguishing.

bunkers of 'Baustärke A', some shaped to make the best use of the hillside on which they were built, hence the angled Bau 1 and the curved Bau 5. Most of these bunkers had an annex, or 'Vorbau', comprising overflow offices with walls and ceilings only 50 to 75 centimetres thick.

Two more of these 'Baustärke A' bunkers lay outside the perimeter, one being located in the grounds of a château at Vregny that was developed to house the services of Reichsführer-SS Himmler, and another near a property at Mailly for Foreign Minister von Ribbentrop.

In addition, there were 13 light bunkers in the inner compound to provide additional office space. The design was a protective shell of concrete walls and roof over a standard brick-built hut that Organisation Todt referred to as 'ummantelte Baracken' – concrete-encased huts. The entrances and windows were fitted with armoured doors and shutters but were not gas-proof, and with walls and roof between 50-75 centimetres thick, these bunkers offered limited protection, the Organisation Todt considering them only 'splittersicher' – shrapnel proof. The size of these light bunkers varied from 23 to 45 metres, by either 11.4 or 14 metres, and each provided 10 to 20 rooms with a central corridor.

In the inner compound there were also three large bunkers housing generators, eight standard command or shelter bunkers, about ten large wooden huts, and odd buildings like garages and workshops. The bunkers housing generators were built to 'Baustärke B' specification having the roof and walls two metres thick. A French report drawn up in the early 1950s explains that poor-quality timber had been used in the construction of the

Men of the 602nd Engineer Battalion soon came across the abandoned German headquarters and at Vauxaillon, near the northern entrance of the railway tunnel, they took this shot of a Type 108A ammunition storage bunker. There were two bunkers of this type close to one another and both still stand in an open field in front of the Vauxaillon railway station. (USNA and ATB)

Trees now hide most of the 'W 2' bunkers from aerial observation but the pair of bunkers at Vauxaillon show up clearly. Type 108A ammunition bunkers measured 16.8 by 18 metres, with walls and ceiling three metres thick, and featured two storage rooms, each six by three metres. The road seen on the left alongside the railway line is the original German concrete road. (Google)

Two 'Baustärke A' bunkers were built outside the FHQu compound. One was at Mailly, 15 kilometres to the north-east, for Foreign Minister von Ribbentrop and his staff.

wooden buildings and that these were already in poor condition. It stated that repair was impossible and that they should be demolished yet the large hut, No. 10b, still survived till the mid-1970s.

One notable timber construction was the 'Teehaus' or 'Kasino' on the hillside about 200 metres from the Führerbunker. It had two dining rooms and a bar and served as the Officers' Mess. Known as the 'Green Chalet' during the post-war era, it ended up in poor shape and was finally demolished in 1986. Another wooden chalet stood near the railway line by the southern entrance. Its purpose is not known although it might have been the office of the security services. In the 1970s it was known as the 'White Chalet' or the 'Finnish Chalet' and was used by the French Army to house high-ranking guests. It, too, was removed in the 1980s.

There were also about 70 wooden huts distributed throughout the area to serve as barracks for the Flak gun crews. Generally, they were provided with earth banks for blast protection. Most of these were also demolished in the 1950s, the remainders in the 1970s or 1980s, but in many places the protecting walls still survive today.

The FHQu compound was defended by an outer belt of defences comprising a total of about 155 bunkers of various type and function in a radius of a few kilometres around the headquarters. Around 80 of these were personnel quarters for the troops and 60 were bunkers armed with machine guns. Most were in open 'Tobruk' positions (a concrete foxhole occupied by a two-man team) but there were ten Type 98A and three Type 105A machine gun bunkers, like this one at Neuville.

The headquarters compound was defended by an outer belt of defences comprising around 60 bunkers with machine guns, most in open 'Tobruk'-type positions, but some with either a steel plate embrasure or armoured cupola. There were also personnel shelters and numerous ammunition stores. 'W 2' was defended against air attack by seven heavy Flak batteries and around five light/medium batteries. The heavies each had six 105mm guns plus two or three 20mm guns and a 60cm searchlight, and the light and

These defence bunkers were mostly left untouched by the later French and NATO troops occupying the compound and original German markings can still be seen in many of them today. This armoured cupola on top of a Type 99A bunker can still be seen at Margival, off the right-hand side of the road, about 100 metres beyond the turning which climbs past the entrance to the FHQu compound. For the technically minded, the cupola is a Type 407P9 with three firing slits.

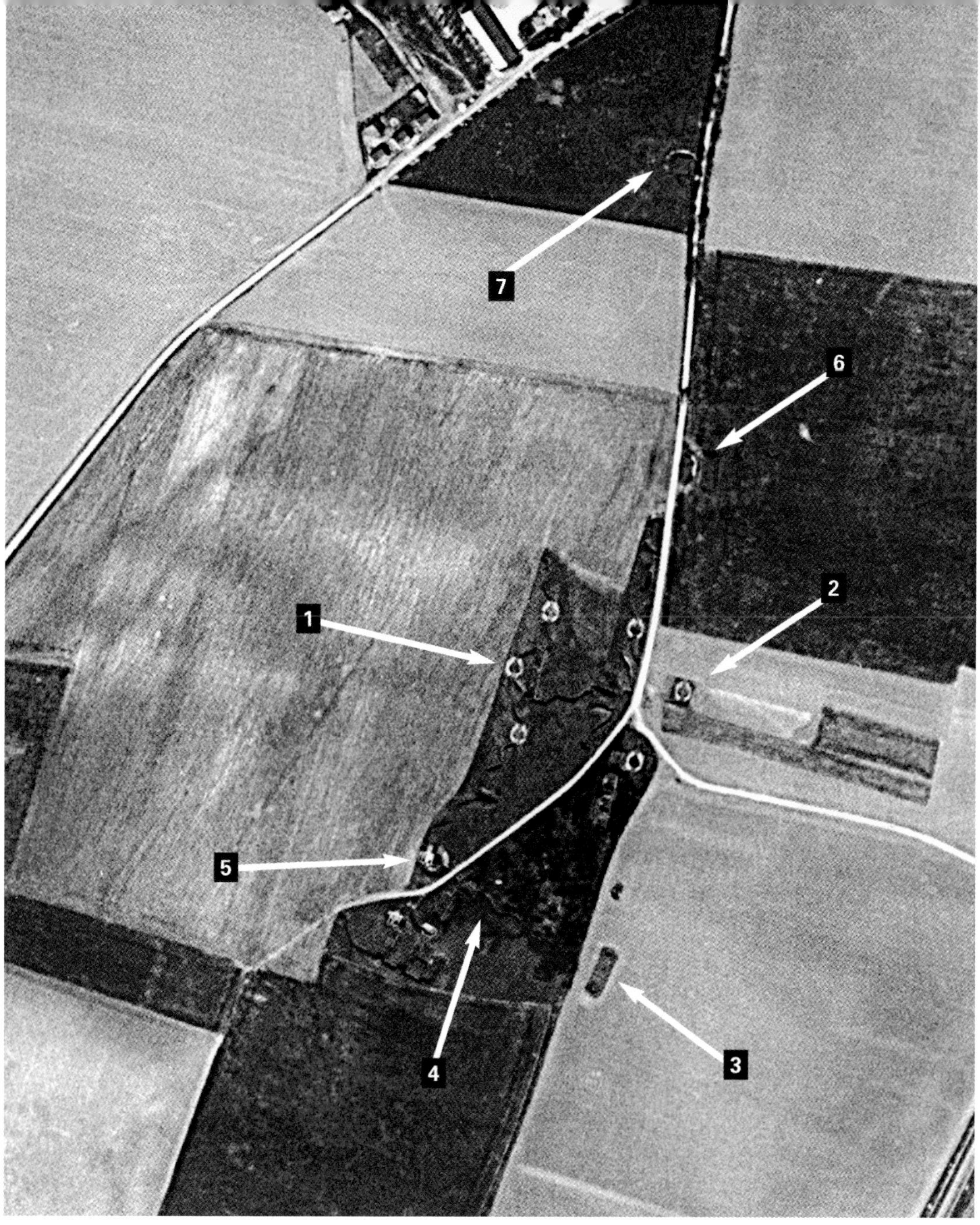

Seven heavy Flak batteries defended FHQu 'W 2' against air attack, each having six 105mm guns plus two or three 20mm guns and one 60cm searchlight. The weapons were installed in concrete emplacements, with associated bunkers being provided for personnel and ammunition as well as shelters for generators. In addition, each position comprised about ten wooden huts that served as barracks for the gun crews. The heavy Flak battery just south of the village of Laffaux featured six 105mm gun positions of Type 103A – at [1] and [2] – and three 20mm gun positions of Type L1 (two at [3] and one at [4]). It also had one Type 426 communication post [5] and one Type 407 ammunition depot [6]. A Type 621 personnel shelter lies north of the battery [7] and another at the right end of the zig-zagging trench in the centre of the 105mm gun positions. The wooden huts had already been demolished by the time this aerial photo was taken in 1949 although the excavations in which they were sited to give protection still showed up. Three of them stood side by side below and left of the battery, with a third slightly above; four were in line just under the fork of the inverted Y-shaped tracks; one was at the left end of the zig-zag trench within the circle of gun positions; and one was situated just above the circle, by the side of the incoming track. (IGN)

The heavy Flak battery located near the village of Moisy is remarkably well preserved, though now totally enveloped by farmland. These are two of the Type 103A gun positions.

One of the three 20mm gun positions of Type L1. All in all, the gun crews and associated searchlight units of the Flak batteries defending FHQu 'W 2' amounted to about 1,800 men.

medium batteries were mostly armed with 37mm guns, 12 guns each, and some with 20mm guns.

A FÜHRERHAUPTQUARTIER FOR ONE DAY

On June 15, 1944, having received yet another unrealistic order from Berlin to free seven panzer divisions for offensive action without weakening any part of the front, the Commander-in-Chief West, Generalfeldmarschall von Rundstedt, requested that either the Chief of the Operations Staff of OKW, Generaloberst Jodl, or his deputy, General der Artillerie Warlimont, come to France to discuss the future conduct of operations in more realistic terms. Instead, Hitler decided to come in person to meet with von Rundstedt and Generalfeldmarschall Rommel, the commander of Heeresgruppe B.

Hitler flew from Salzburg to Metz in a Focke-Wulf Condor with an escort of three fighters in the evening of June 16 together with Jodl, Schmundt, and a few staff officers. Landing at Frescaty, near Metz, Hitler was driven to Margival early next morning. The party was greeted at the Teehaus, the wooden chalet on the hillside that served as the Officers' Mess. Von Rundstedt and Rommel then arrived with their Chiefs-of-Staff, General Günther Blumentritt and Generalleutnant Hans Speidel. The meeting then began at 9.30 a.m. in the large conference room of Bunker No. 1.

Unfortunately, no photographs appear to have been taken that day and the only surviving minutes are those noted by Major i. G. Arthur von

On the evening on June 16, 1944, an unexpected telephone call ordered Generalfeldmarschall Erwin Rommel, commander of Heeresgruppe B, and his Chief-of-Staff Generalleutnant Hans Speidel (both pictured here in April 1944) to report to 'Battle Headquarters Wolfsschlucht 2' at Margival at 9 a.m. on June 17 to give a report in person to Hitler. Generalfeldmarschall Gerd von Rundstedt, the Commander-in-Chief in the West, received the same instruction. (BA)

The meeting began at 9.30 a.m. in the conference room in the 'Vorbau' of Bau 1 and lasted till 12.30 p.m. when lunch was served in the nearby Teehaus. The investigation team from the 602nd Engineer Camouflage Battalion photographed the conference room in September 1944, simply captioning it as 'interior of one of the headquarters buildings'. But for the horseman sculpture on the chimney breast, the room was quite sparsely furnished, with a nondescript table, chairs, bookshelves, and a lamp standard that might be found in any house. (USNA)

Pierre Rhode and Werner Sünkel were lucky to be able to visit the bunker in the 1980s when the conference room was still in fairly good shape, though the equestrian statue had by then already been broken by vandals. In 2007 reckless fools lit a fire in this bunker and the conflagration which raged for hours completely gutted the interior.
(P. Rhode and W. Sünkel)

Ekesparre of the staff of Heeresgruppe B. However, both Blumentritt and Speidel later wrote down their recollections of the day. Speidel described how 'Hitler looked pale and sleepless, playing nervously with his glasses and an array of coloured pencils which he held between his fingers. He sat hunched upon a stool while the field marshals stood. His hypnotic powers seemed to have waned.'

Following a curt and frosty greeting, Hitler expressed his dissatisfaction with the attempt to counter the Allied landings, finding fault with the local commanders. He ordered that fortress Cherbourg be held at any cost. For their part, the field-marshals sought to obtain freedom of action, including permission to draw reserves at will from coastal areas not immediately threatened by invasion. They also recommended certain withdrawals in order to shorten their lines and concentrate their forces.

To this Hitler made no direct reply but instead changed the subject to claim that the tide would soon be turned by the V-weapons. Introducing General Erich Heinemann, the commander of the LXV. Armeekorps that had been formed specifically to command the V-weapon offensive, Hitler warmly thanked him for the successful opening of the campaign against England. 'The impression arose', wrote Blumentritt later, 'that Hitler diverted himself by this means from the bitter knowledge of the real situation'. The meeting broke up about half past midday without any decisions having been made.

Lunch was served in the Teehaus. Speidel: 'A one-dish meal at which Hitler bolted a heaped plate of rice and vegetables after it had been previously tasted for him. Pills ranged around his place and he took them in turn. Two SS men stood guard behind his chair.' After the meal, a presentation was given to publicise the introduction of the V1 campaign that had begun on June 13.

The conference was resumed after lunch when Rommel dared to suggest that it was time to come to terms with the Western Allies. Jodl later recalled how Hitler heard him out in silence before sharply retorting: 'That is a

On June 17, Hitler, von Rundstedt, Rommel, and their staffs had lunch at 12.30 p.m. in the Teehaus, a large wooden chalet on the hillside. It served as an officers' club and contained a large and a smaller dining room, as well as a bar with a tiled stove which contemporaries remembered as very beautiful. Speidel later recounted how there was a remarkable distant view of Soissons Cathedral from there. Having become dilapidated, the Teehaus was demolished in 1986, but fortunately *After the Battle* took this photo of it in 1977.

question which is not your responsibility. You will have to leave that to me.' An air raid warning was then sounded and Hitler and the rest of the delegates entered the shelter at the side of the bunker where they remained for an hour, hardly a word being spoken. They emerged some time before 3 p.m. Speidel wrote that 'before the conference ended, Hitler's chief adjutant, Generalleutnant Schmundt, apparently impressed by Rommel's repeated warnings that the High Command had to have first-hand knowledge of the front, asked the Chief-of-Staff of Heeresgruppe B to prepare for a visit on June 19 by Hitler to La Roche-Guyon or some other suitable headquarters'.

Once the two field-marshals had departed, Hitler and his party carried out a short inspection tour of the headquarters before leaving for Germany later that evening having suddenly cancelled the meeting planned for the 19th. There is some doubt as to the precise route they took to return to Germany. Von Below said that the party returned by car to Metz, arriving in the early morning, from where they flew to Salzburg, but local unsubstantiated accounts claim that the party took off from a local airfield, Juvincourt or Laon-Couvron.

In his book *Invasion 1944: Rommel and the Normandy Campaign* published in 1950, Speidel stated that it was the crash of a rogue V1 nearby that alarmed the Führer and his staff and precipitated their departure. However, this is incorrect for the V1 incident occurred during the early hours of June 17 before the Hitler party arrived. The proof is given in a telex from Jodl to the LXV. Armeekorps later that day: 'On June 17, about 0430 hours, what was probably a FZG 76 crashed about two kilometres from Camp W 2. The remains found at the site of the impact have been impounded by Criminal-Inspector Schmidt, RSD W 2. The LXV. Armeekorps will immediately start an investigation and report the result to the chief of the WFSt.'

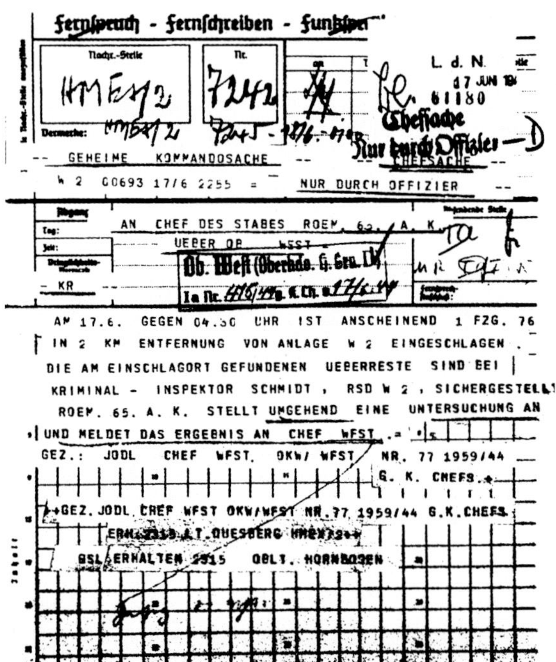

Fernspruch - Fernschreiben - Funkspruch

Nachr.-Stelle: HMEX 2 Nr.: 7242

L. d. N. 17 JUN 1944 61180

Chefsache

Nur durch Offizier

-- GEHEIME KOMMANDOSACHE -- CHEFSACHE --

W 2 00693 17/6 2255 = NUR DURCH OFFIZIER --

AN CHEF DES STABES ROEM. 65. A. K.

UEBER OB WEST

Ob. West (Oberkdo. H. Gru. D)

Ia Nr. 4416/44 g. K. Ch. v. 17.6.44

-- KR --

AM 17.6. GEGEN 04.30 UHR IST ANSCHEINEND 1 FZG. 76 IN 2 KM ENTFERNUNG VON ANLAGE W 2 EINGESCHLAGEN. DIE AM EINSCHLAGORT GEFUNDENEN UEBERRESTE SIND BEI KRIMINAL - INSPEKTOR SCHMIDT, RSD W 2, SICHERGESTELLT. ROEM. 65. A. K. STELLT UMGEHEND EINE UNTERSUCHUNG AN UND MELDET DAS ERGEBNIS AN CHEF WFST. =

GEZ.: JODL CHEF WFST. OKW/WFST NR. 77 1959/44 G. K. CHEFS. +

+GEZ. JODL CHEF WFST OKW/WFST NR. 77 1959/44 G.K.CHEFS.

ERH. 2319 LT. QUESBERG HMEX 2++

BSL ERHALTEN 2315 OBLT. HORNBOSEN

This is the telex sent on the evening of June 17 by Generaloberst Alfred Jodl: 'On June 17, about 0430 hours, what was probably a FZG 76 crashed about two kilometres from Camp W 2'. The time is in Central European Summer Time which in June 1944 was GMT + 2.

FZG 76 was a code-name for the V1; RSD W 2 stands for Reichssicherheitsdienst at W 2, the Reichssicherheitsdienst being the security service which provided protection for high Nazi officials; and the chief of the WFSt was Jodl himself.

Although Hitler's reason for cancelling the meeting at La Roche-Guyon has not been recorded, possibly he was not in a mood to continue the argument with the two field-marshals, and Rommel's suggestion for a political solution was the last straw. Talking about this meeting to Speer on his return to Obersalzberg, Hitler told him how Rommel had lost his nerve and become pessimistic. He also commented that 'Wolfsschlucht 2' was not safe, 'lying as it was in the middle of France infested by Partisans'.

THE CAPTURE OF 'WOLFSSCHLUCHT 2'

The 'W 2' installations were finally used as a command post for Heeresgruppe B that re-established itself at Margival on August 19 after having pulled out from La Roche-Guyon under American artillery fire earlier that morning. When the US VII Corps launched their attack from the Melun bridgehead on the River Seine on August 26, it quickly unhinged the LVIII. Panzerkorps, and by the 28th, the 3rd Armored Division was speeding through Château-Thierry and Soissons. As a result, Generalfeldmarschall Model (Commander-in-Chief West and commander of Heeresgruppe B since mid-August) and the staff of the Heeresgruppe B headquarters

This V1 is believed to have been launched from a ramp at Vignacourt, near Abbeville, but instead of flying north, went off course and flew 120 kilometres south-east before crashing close to the Saint-Guislain farm at Allemant, about four kilometres east of the Führerhauptquartier. The terrain was marshy and the impact crater had soon disappeared. Absolutely no trace of it is visible at the position circled on this aerial photograph taken by the French Institut Géographique National in 1949. (IGN)

The author had the witness of Bernard Adam, a farmer living in the nearby village of Vaudesson, who heard and saw the pulse of the missile's engine in the sky, then the silence before the explosion, less than two kilometres from where he stood. Another witness was André Leleu, who ran the Saint-Guislain farm, remembers the tremendous shock of the V1 exploding just a few hundred metres from the farm, leaving an eight-metre-wide crater in the marshy ground. He was checking for damage to the farm buildings when German troops arrived within ten minutes or so after the crash, asking where the 'aircraft' had crashed. They started to systematically collect what else remained of the missile.

quit Margival late that evening having been operational there for just ten days. There was no time to destroy the installations and they were all left intact save for the radio station on the top of the hill. Although the garrison withdrew in good time, taking with them the 20mm and 37mm guns, the heavier 105mm weapons had to be spiked and abandoned where they were.

Elements of the 3rd Armored Division reached and passed through Margival on the afternoon of August 29, en route to Laon. Following the leading armour, the 1st Infantry Division cleared Soissons, finding two trains standing in the station, one of them loaded with food. 'First Division messes for several days were enlivened by Westphalia hams and noodles, and tinned asparagus and some of the best canned cherries that ever dazzled a soldier who had seen nothing like that for months, and would not see anything like that for still longer'.

North-west of Soissons, off the main route of advance, infantrymen then came upon 'the almost unbelievable creation at Margival, the newly completed and never occupied headquarters for the German Commander in the West'. The divisional historian wrote that: 'It was such a triumph of camouflage that even from a moderate distance at the ground level one would fail to see it, and such a triumph of secrecy in building (by the Organisation Todt) that even the occupants of a nearby village had never seen it and knew only vaguely that some kind of building had been going on with imported workmen. Yet beneath the forest of painted camouflage strips and netting lay broad concrete streets with lamp-posts for night illumination. Beside the road lay the well-designed buildings of reinforced concrete walls reaching far below ground-level, roofed with armour comfortably and even luxuriously furnished for the great number of staff officers who were to have offices and quarters in this model headquarters. The council room designed for von Rundstedt with its map-cases and huge table, perfectly lighted, almost made one wish that the war would halt around here long enough to permit its use by the Division. Fire extinguishers were in their places, engravings on the neat walls (labels on the backs were invariably those of looted art-shops in Paris), comfortable work chairs and easy chairs in each officer's room and (model of German thoroughness) in each wardrobe a bootjack. About the edge of Margival were defence-post pillboxes but for precaution's sake no large anti-aircraft installations: those we later saw on the surrounding hills. It was all like a stage set, save for its decidedly permanent character, a truly perfect headquarters completed, by a jocular Fate, just too late to be of any use to its builders.'

A few days later, elements of the 602nd Engineer Camouflage Battalion were sent to Margival to inspect and photograph the various types and techniques of camouflage used by the Germans. The battalion commander, Lieutenant Colonel Robert E. Kearney, sent his report to First Army on October 30: 'The area was observed from the air at altitude of 1,500 and 3,000 feet. It was easy to locate because of the proximity to the railroad tunnel. From these heights the artificial grass, trees and rock were easily discernible. This was due to the colours used. Generally, the materials

On August 25, the US XX Corps attacked north-eastwards from the bridgehead across the Seine at Melun. The leading troops crossed the Marne River on the 28th, wheeled eastwards, and by noon on the 31st were at Verdun and across the Meuse. The US VII Corps attacked in turn on the 26th with the 3rd Armored Division leading, and on the 29th the division's Combat Command B crossed the Aisne at Soissons. They were now just eight kilometres from 'Wolfsschlucht 2' which had been abandoned by the Germans just a short time before. Here, an M5 light tank of CCB crosses the Place de la République in Melun, with a Sherman and Jeep in the background. The tanks were heading for the Aisne bridge which lies about 500 metres off to the right. (USNA)

Looking north-west across the square from the Avenue de Reims today.

were darker than the surrounding foliage. Texturing however was good, and the camouflage blended well on photographs. The material used for the dummy roofs gave an excellent imitation of tile. It was also noted that although a great deal of excavating had been done, no spoil was in evidence. It must have been hauled away, or added to a hillside and covered with sod. No signs of construction work were visible.

In many places near the 'W 2' compound – such as at Laffaux, Neuville and Vauxaillon – the Germans used ancient underground quarries to store equipment, supplies, and food. They concreted the entrance for some distance, and sometimes installed Decauville narrow railway tracks to service the interior. This is one of the three ventilation and escape exits built by the Germans for the quarry at Vauxaillon.

'In general, the camouflage measures taken throughout this area were excellent. Although in many cases the artificial materials were evident, neither photography nor direct observation revealed the nature nor the exact location of the structures being camouflaged, and accurate observation of the installations would have been difficult.'

The report also noted how each end of the tunnel was hidden under camouflage covering over the tracks to a distance of about 150 metres.

American forces occupied the HQ for some months but when war ended it was used to house displaced persons, Italians, Czechs, and Yugoslavs, and finally elements of Polish troops who had served with the British Army. Some time later, Margival was used as a base to assemble and train Indo-Chinese troops as France was then becoming involved in the war in Indo-China. Later female units of the French Army were trained there.

Following NATO's North Atlantic Council decision in September 1950 to create an integrated European defence force, the establishment of SHAPE (Supreme Headquarters Allied Powers Europe) proceeded quickly and in April 1951 General Dwight D. Eisenhower was appointed Supreme Allied Commander Europe, with Field-Marshal Bernard L. Montgomery as Deputy. In July, a brand-new headquarters was inaugurated for SHAPE at Rocquencourt, near Versailles, south-west of Paris. Subordinated commands for Northern and Southern Europe were established in Oslo and Naples respectively and the Central Europe command was established at Fontainebleau, south of Paris. Ensuring the survivability of senior command staffs in a nuclear environment was an immediate concern and Margival's extensive infrastructure was soon chosen to serve as a primary static war headquarters for the Central Europe command. A considerable amount of work was undertaken to renovate and modernise the old bunkers of the former 'W 2' HQ, but few new buildings were constructed. Extensive communication links were established, including in the late 1950s the tropospheric network then being built across Western Europe to link SHAPE with its subordinate commands.

By a queer twist of fate, General Speidel then returned at Margival. After the war, he had served for some time as Professor of Modern History at Tübingen University, his book referred to above being published in October 1950. One month earlier, the three Western occupation powers – Britain, France, and the United States – had accepted in principle that West Germany could contribute military forces to the security of Europe and Speidel became involved in the development and creation of the Bundeswehr. West Germany joined the North Atlantic Treaty Organisation (NATO) in 1955 and in April 1957 Speidel was appointed Commander Allied Land Forces Central Europe. In June, he was promoted to four-star rank just as the first three German divisions joined NATO forces. He immediately brought new perspectives, challenging the Allies to think innovatively about the relationship between conventional and nuclear forces in the conduct of land operations. Speidel remained at this post until September 1963, an impressive achievement considering he had been a general under Hitler only 15 years before!

However, the Margival complex soon proved to be a heavy burden on the NATO budget. Despite costly efforts to make the HQ adequate in an NBC environment, being above ground, it never proved to be fully satisfactory. Also, the extensive site required a large guard force to secure the perimeter, and the demands for electricity, water and maintenance proved to be difficult to satisfy.

In 1966 Président Charles de Gaulle decided to withdraw from the integrated military command of NATO as he wanted France to be able to act independently (although the country was to remain a member of the organisation and of the North Atlantic Pact). Consequently, NATO vacated its former headquarters in Rocquencourt and Fontainebleau in April 1967 to relocate in Belgium, the personnel at Margival following in June. (It would not be until 1977, ten years after having evacuated Margival, that NATO Central Europe command possessed an adequate headquarters for war operations, this being the underground facility code-named 'Erwin' at Boerfink, near Kaiserslautern, in Germany.)

From 1968 the Margival facilities were used as a training centre for French commandos, an obvious reminder of this period being the 'village' built in the 1980s at the junction at the bottom of Bau (Building) 1 for practising street-fighting.

The commandos left in 1985 and from then on, the camp served occasionally for manoeuvres by the 67ème Régiment d'Infanterie which was based at Soissons. In 1987 there were talks of constructing a hospital there for the German army and, although money was spent in the early 1990s to sanitise and update the facilities, the former Hitler headquarters finally closed in July 1993. From then on, although the area remained off-limits for individual access, much looting, theft, and mindless vandalism took place.

In 2005 the whole site was offered back to the communities of Laffaux, Margival and Neuville whose land had been taken in 1939, each village taking back its former territory.

The 'ASW2' association has worked hard for two decades to clean, restore, and secure the former 'Wolfsschlucht 2', and they now manage tours of the site, and of bunkers they have rehabilitated. Among them are three of the large bunkers on the hill: bunker no. 8, one of the 'ummantelte Baracken', cleaned and restored; the immense bunker no. 5, telecommunications centre, cleaned but not yet restored; and bunker no. 1, Hitler's bunker, of which only the 'Baustärke A' part is visited (set on fire by vandals the Vorbau is not accessible in complete safety).

In addition, ASW2 restored several small bunkers, such as no. 11, a type 502 (Doppelgruppenunterstand), no. 17, a Type 608 (Gefechtsstand) and no. 23b, a Type 621 (Gruppenunterstand). They also restored defence bunkers, such as a Type 105A machine gun bunker at Neuville, and a Type 601 anti-tank gun bunker at Pont-Rouge, just south of Margival.

When most of the FHQu have been destroyed, many carefully erased, it is a chance to have access to the immense 'Wolfsschlucht 2', the largest of the FHQu to survive in good condition (in the East, destroyed by German engineers, FHQu 'Wolfschanze' is in ruins). Up to date information can be found at **https://ravinduloup2.wixsite.com/asw2/w2**.

FÜHRERHAUPTQUARTIER 'WOLFSSCHLUCHT 3'

AS THE ORGANISATION TODT was constructing FHQu 'Wolfsschlucht 2' at Margival, works were underway in parallel at Saint-Rimay near Montoire-sur-le-Loir, 15 kilometres west of Vendôme, for the construction of a second headquarters for Hitler in France, code-named 'Wolfsschlucht 3'.

On May 29, 1942, Hitler issued his Directive No. 42 covering instructions for operations against unoccupied France and the Iberian Peninsula. 'The development of the situation in unoccupied France, or in the French possessions in North Africa, may render it necessary in the future to occupy the whole of French territory. Likewise, we must reckon on possible enemy attempts to seize the Iberian Peninsula, which will call for immediate counter-measures on our part.'

In accordance with the preoccupation of the German high command with a possible second front in the West in the Iberian Peninsula, the decision was taken in the spring of 1942 to construct a second Führer headquarters in France. The new one was to be located deeper in France than 'Wolfsschlucht 2' already being built at Margival.

It appears that someone remembered the tunnel at Saint-Rimay which had been earmarked to shelter Hitler's personal train when it stopped at Montoire-sur-le-Loir to meet Marshal Pétain in October 1940. As this might form an ideal location, on June 22, 1942, a team headed by the commander of the Führerhauptquartier, Oberst Thomas, arrived at Montoire to carry out a detailed survey of the tunnel. Available records do not state who took the decision to go ahead and build the second FHQu at Saint-Rimay, and when, but everything points to Oberst Thomas giving the orders following his survey.

Construction of 'Wolfsschlucht 3' started in June 1942. However, Speer, the Minister of Armaments, still seemed unaware that construction had begun when, at the end of September, he sent a note to Dorsch, the head of the Organisation Todt, ordering him 'not to begin building a second FHQu establishment (in France) without my express permission'. Even so, on October 23, Oberst Engel inspected both 'Wolfsschlucht 2' and 'Wolfsschlucht 3' with Schmelcher and his deputy Müller.

'Oberbauleitung Wolfsschlucht 3' was formally established under the auspices of OT-Einsatzgruppe West. Baurat Simon was assigned the work, assisted by architect Luis Gerland of Schmelcher's FHQu building group.

The entire population of Cherchenois, the hamlet that lay close to the heart of the planned headquarters at the north-eastern entrance of the

When Hitler met Maréchal Philippe Pétain, the head of the Vichy government of France, at Montoire-su le-Loir in October 1940, the organiser of the diplomatic tour chose a useful shelter for the Führer's special train a a railway tunnel at Saint-Rimay, four kilometres to the north-east. Two yea later, this same tunnel became the sit of Führerhauptquartier 'Wolfsschluch 3', the most western of Hitler's headquarters. These men of Infanteri Regiment 173 of the 87. Infanterie-Division then billeted in Montoire wer pictured in front of the ruins of its medieval castle. (M. Doucet)

tunnel, was evacuated, and farmers were provided with passes to enable them to return to work their fields, though they still had to be accompanied by a German guard. Other habitations in the area, even those close to the southern entrance of the tunnel, were not affected.

Like 'Wolfsschlucht 2' at Margival, it was the existence of a suitable railway tunnel that settled the decision to build 'Wolfsschlucht 3' at Saint-Rimay. Baurat Simon commissioned geological experts to survey the ridge through which the tunnel ran and they reported back in February. They explained that the tunnel had been bored through chalky lime. This meant that there was a risk of deep penetration from shells of large-calibre guns and heavy bombs, although shells would meet high friction in this soft chalk lime which might decrease their ability to penetrate deeply. Also, because of

From May 1942, the unit of the Organisation Todt involved in the construction of 'Wolfsschlucht 3' established its headquarters in the Château de Prépatour, midway between Saint-Rimay and Vendôme.
(M. Doucet)

the softness of the lime, the pressure of exploding shells would be dissipated better than in hard rock.

Referring to a report by the Inspekteur der Landbefestigungen West (Inspector of Land Fortifications in the West), a department of the Ob. West headquarters, which recommended that the material above the tunnel had to be at least 30 metres thick to give adequate protection, the survey pointed out that only the central section of the tunnel had the required cover. (The maximum coverage of about 41 metres was at a point 150 metres from the eastern entrance.) At the western end, the 30-metre cover was lacking for a length of 81 metres from the entrance, and for 36 metres at the eastern end. Also, an abandoned quarry above the tunnel at the western end additionally weakened the protection. Because of the inadequate cover, the report

These three men belong to the Reichsarbeitsdienst (RAD, Reich Labour Service). Two are Obertruppführers but the rank of the third man cannot be seen. They wore the RAD paramilitary uniform with a large swastika armband and the RAD badge on the cap. (M. Doucet)

Another shot in this series of photos shows the unit badge worn on the upper left sleeve, identifying the men as belonging to RAD-Abteilung 364, a unit from the XXXVI. Arbeitsgau of the RAD based in south-eastern Austria. (M. Doucet)

For decades, the site of 'Wolfsschlucht 3' remained unknown and as late as 1989, Dr Richard Raiber, author of *Guide to Hitler's Headquarters*, was misled to assume that 'Wolfsschlucht 3' was another code-name for FHQu 'Brunhilde' in Lorraine. It was only in the early 1990s that the site of Saint-Rimay was finally recognised for what it was: the former Führerhauptquartier 'Wolfsschlucht 3'. The decision to build a Führerhauptquartier at Saint-Rimay was influenced by the existence of a railway tunnel which could shelter Hitler's personal train. Close by the southern entrance to the tunnel the Saint-Rimay station is now closed, and the railway crossing automated, but the place remains remarkably unchanged after three-quarters of a century. The tunnel is so perfectly straight that one can see right through to the northern exit in the distance.

recommended reinforcement of the tunnel at each entrance and both should be provided with fortified porches.

However, the OT engineers decided against trying to strengthen the weak lengths at each end with reinforced concrete, and instead they planned to seal the tunnel with massive armoured doors. These would be positioned either side of the central section, at 40 metres and 35 metres respectively from each entrance. Each hinged door was to measure five metres by five metres, recesses being provided in the tunnel wall to fit the door when open. Another recess facing it was made to seal the door when it closed. Loco drivers were to stop their train in between the two doors, and these would be shut if an air raid alarm was sounded.

The German surveyors found that both ends of the tunnel lacked the required cover of rock above it to give adequate protection and the Organisation Todt engineers therefore sealed the central part with massive armoured doors. The Führer's personal train was to halt in between the two. The two doors survived post-war modernisation of the railway network and can still be seen, in perfect state, tucked away in their recesses in the side of the tunnel. Each hinged door measures five metres by five metres, with four-centimetre-thick armoured plate fixed to large 'I-beams'. A cross beam in the middle reinforces the construction, as does an additional X-shaped structure. This shot shows how one recess was dug into the tunnel wall on one side to fit the door when open, while another recess in the facing wall receives it when it is closed.

A report by Schmelcher in 1944 covered 'work on an existing tunnel and construction of a station platform as a shelter for a Sonderzug' and 'construction of a bunker for the Führer and a meeting bunker and construction of huts'. It pointed out that these constructions were only for the FHQu, hence, contrary to what was done at 'Wolfsschlucht 2', nothing was to be built to house services of the Oberkommando des Heeres (OKH, Army High Command) or the Reichsführer-SS.

Unfortunately, the report does not include a plan of 'Wolfsschlucht 3' and no other original plan of this Führerhauptquartier appears to have survived. Also, no photos of the headquarters taken during the war have been discovered, which is no surprise for one can understand that the Germans would have banned all photography for security reasons.

The Schmelcher report stated that the work had used 9,000 cubic metres of concrete and provided 7,000 square metres of useful space.

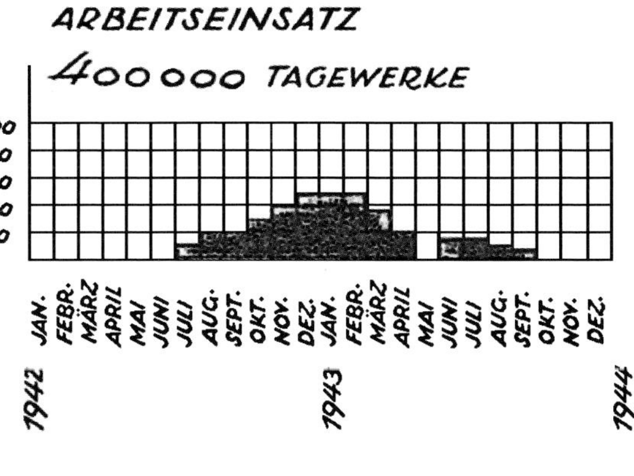

Work on the new Führerhauptquartier began in the spring of 1942, the Organisation Todt building two massive bunkers and some 100 other constructions around the Saint-Rimay railway tunnel. This sketch from the Schmelcher report issued in November 1944 shows precisely how work started in June 1942 with a workforce of 500. It then increased to 1,000 in July, 1,500 in September and 2,000 in October, to reach a peak of 2,500 in November, December and January 1943. Work stopped in April to resume in May, finally ceasing in August, although it is possible that this final five-month period just involved the work to dismantle the site. The report indicates that construction of 'Wolfsschlucht 3' had involved 400,000 working days.

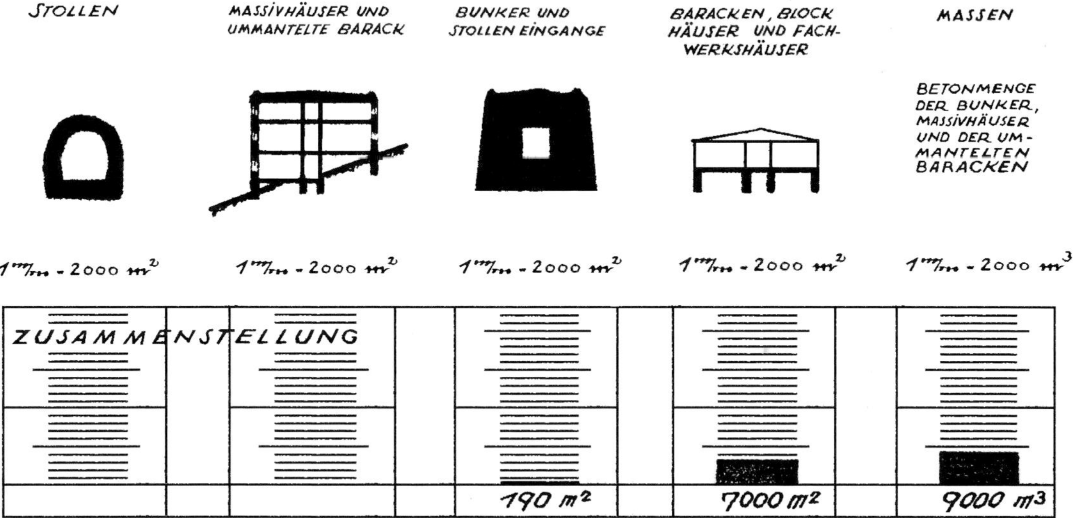

The document states that the work had provided 190 square metres of useful space in strong bunkers, 7,000 square metres in wooden huts and had used 9,000 cubic metres of concrete. It indicates that neither Stollen (tunnels), nor Massivhäuser (concrete-reinforced buildings) or ummantelte Baracken (concrete-reinforced huts) were built on the site.

However, only 190 square metres covering two bunkers had been built to 'Baustärke A' standard, most of the surface buildings being wooden huts. Some were to house services in the centre of the compound, with additional accommodation for the Flak and security forces all over the place.

Work started in June 1942 with a workforce of 500, this being increased to 1,000 in July and then, after an inspection to check on progress by Oberbauleiter Müller in October, to 2,500. Most of the labour force was provided by French building firms contracted to the Organisation Todt, and local people recollect it included French, Belgian, Dutch, and Italian workers. Some of them were quartered in the Marescot Barracks at Montoire, commuting by train to Saint-Rimay, while others were lodged either at Vendôme, being brought in by rail or road, or billeted locally.

The Germans conscripted local manpower to provide the necessary transportation, and each of the villages in the neighbourhood – Thoré-la-

A series of aerial photos taken in April 1949 gives an early post-war view. This is the hamlet of Cherchenois covering the area by the headquarters compound. The white rectangles indicate the sites of the huts that were built in 1942 but quickly removed, either by the Germans in 1943 or destroyed by the Americans in 1944. In the top left corner one can see the two large bunkers [1] and [2], the concrete mixing platform [3] and the location of the huts that were built on either side of the manor house. In the centre, the huts were built on a slope with retaining walls on the lower side, most having a cellar that housed the heating installation. The last hut in this series (at the right-hand end) housed the soldier's mess. At the bottom is the series of huts built along the edge of the wood, hidden under the trees. On the extreme left of the row, a four-metre-deep excavation provided a sheltered platform for a large hut, the concrete walls all around being taller than the hut. The excavation is still there today (the tip of wood pointing downward at bottom centre) but nearly filled up with detritus and covered by trees and bushes. In the top right corner, close to the railway line, were the carpentry shop [4] and the material depot [5] where supplies and equipment, particularly the bags of cement, were stored after being unloaded from the nearby railway. (IGN)

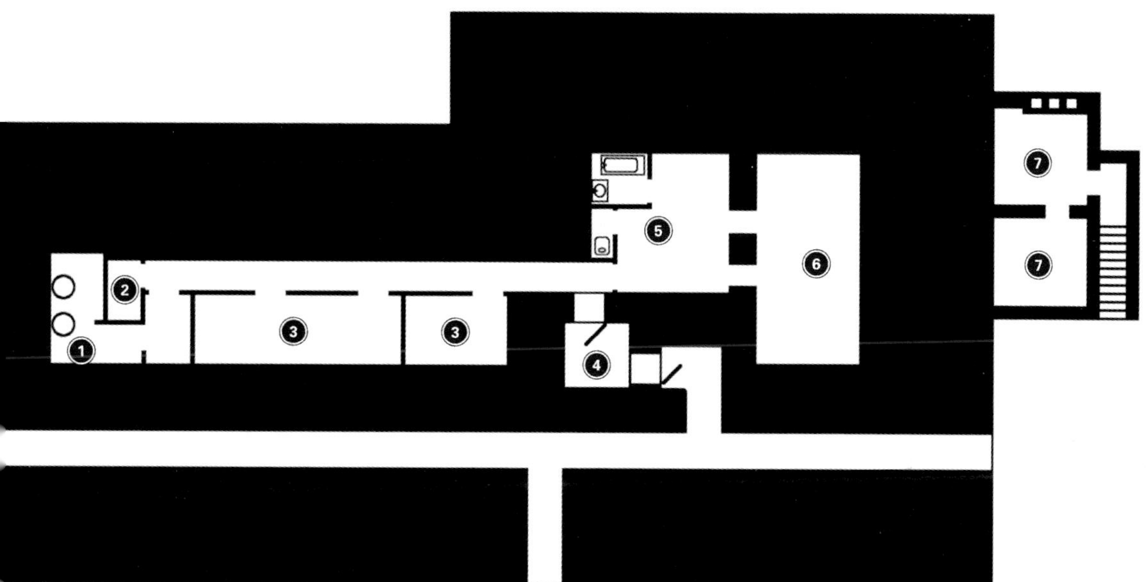

The Organisation Todt report makes it clear that the large 'Baustärke A' bunker on the right-hand side of the tunnel's northern entrance was reserved 'for the Führer'. The long corridor that ran along the whole length of the bunker had three entrances, a gas-lock giving the only access to the interior. From left to right were situated the engine room [1] with two Type HES 2.4 air purifiers; a toilet [2]; offices [3]; the gas-lock with its pair of gas-proof armoured doors [4]; the bathroom with a tub and another toilet [5], and Hitler's personal quarters [6]. Outside the bunker, two cellars [7] housed the coal-fired central heating installation.

Rochette, Saint-Rimay and Houssay – was required to provide 15 men and a horse-drawn cart for three days. Each man was paid 250 francs a day for his service.

Sand and gravel were produced locally from pits along the Loir River but supplies of cement, steel and timber were brought in by train. To allow for easier loading and unloading of both the labour force and the construction materials, a temporary wooden platform was built alongside the track at the north-eastern end of the tunnel.

The Germans used the airstrips located at Houssay and Villiersfaux, five kilometres south-east of Saint-Rimay, to service the headquarters. These airfields had been prepared in the autumn of 1939 for use by squadrons of the RAF that moved to France with the BEF. However, they saw little use, the Fairey Battles of No. 142 Squadron pulling back to Villiersfaux on June 6, 1940, while No. 150 Squadron was at adjacent Houssay. Both squadrons then operated from there for nine days before leaving for England on June 15. The Germans added some Flak positions around the airfield and a command bunker at La Soivrie.

The bunker is now much overgrown, this is the side entrance.

To the left of the tunnel entrance stands the second bunker of 'Baustärke A', equally impressive as the first, which was described in the Schmelcher report as the 'meeting bunker'. It has two separate entrances in its eastern façade, each with a pair of gas-proof armoured doors.

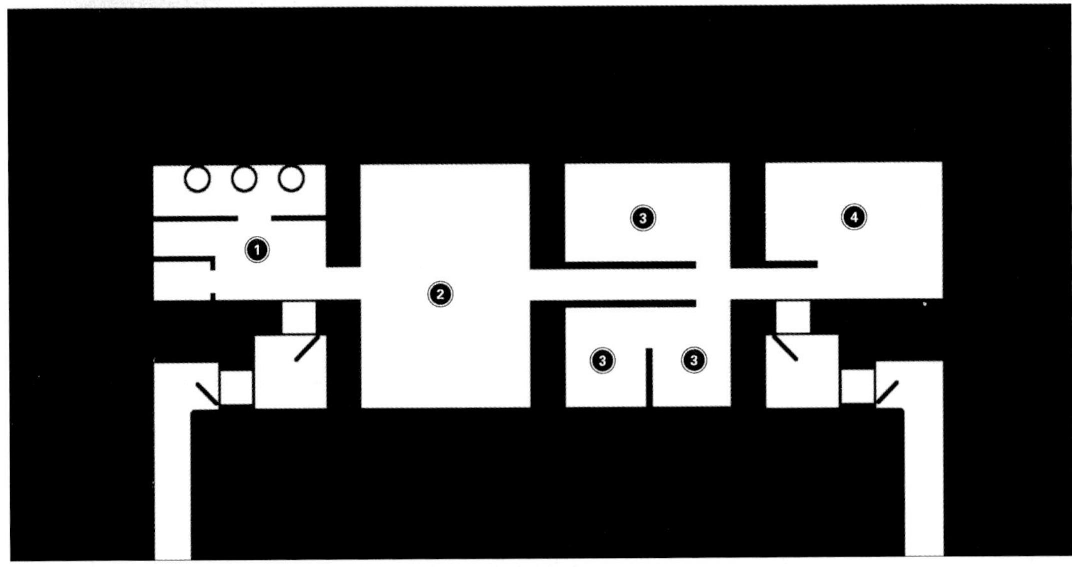

The bunker is divided into four sections. From left to right, the first section [1] housed toilets and the air purification equipment featuring three Type HES 2.4 ventilators/filters. The second room [2], the largest in the bunker measuring six by five metres with no sub-division, would have served as the conference room for Hitler and his generals (although it was never actually used for that purpose). In the next compartment [3] brick walls provided three separate office spaces for adjutants and staff. The last room [4] is symmetrical to that at the other end and the remains of cables in one corner indicate that it most probably housed the electric plant.

The visits of the Führerhauptquartier organised by the Hist'Orius association takes the visitors in the interior of the 'Baustärke A' bunker.

The most impressive constructions at 'Wolfsschlucht 3' were two bunkers built to the 'Baustärke A' standard, i.e. with walls and ceilings comprising 3.5 metres of reinforced concrete. These could withstand the heaviest artillery and direct hits from bombs of up to one ton. Both bunkers were built in the immediate vicinity of the north-eastern entrance of the tunnel.

One was the 'bunker for the Führer' as it was called in Schmelcher's report. It was built on the hillside, slightly higher than the railway track, on the right-hand side of the tunnel's northern entrance (when facing the entrance). A farmhouse that stood on this spot was demolished. The bunker measured 32 metres in length by 18 wide. The entrance to the inner part

At Les Coutils, about one kilometre south-east of the main compound, was the bunker housing the telephone and teleprinter exchange. With concrete walls and roof 70cm thick, it measures 42 metres by 12.6 metres and provided about 20 rooms for the operators on each side of a central corridor on the ground floor, including a dining room and toilets. The basement, six by 12 metres, housed the cables distribution frames and central heating. (IGN)

was through a gas-lock provided by a pair of gas-proof armoured doors, the external door opening onto the long corridor running along the whole length of the bunker, the internal door directly onto the small corridor inside the shelter. It included two toilets and a bathroom with tub. At one end of the bunker was the engine room with two Type HES 2.4 air purifiers (2.4 standing for the volume of air in cubic metres that it could process per minute). This bunker had central heating, the installation being housed in two cellars outside the bunker, one for the solid-fuel boiler, the other for storage of coal, both being accessed via a stairway.

Built on the left-hand side of the tunnel entrance, slightly lower than the railway line track, the second 'Baustärke A' bunker was described as the 'meeting bunker'. This measured 30 metres by 15 metres with two separate entrances with gas-proof armoured doors. The bunker was divided into four sections. One of these, at one end, was for the air purification equipment.

It is unclear whether the internal furnishing of these bunkers was completed when work was suspended in August 1943 but a report dated March 6 that year stated that 'just like in Vinnitsa', the interior walls of the bunkers in 'W 3' must be clad with untreated wood only 'since, for reasons of health, varnished wood is not conducive for the Führer and his staff'. Additional office and service buildings were built close by the two bunkers. Several wooden huts were erected in the hamlet of Cherchenois, while many of the existing buildings were taken over.

A third large bunker was built south-east of the centre to house the telephone and teleprinter exchange. This had thinner walls and roof only 70 centimetres thick. It measured 42 metres by 12.6 metres and provided about 20 rooms on each side of a central corridor on the ground floor and had a large basement. In addition to the telephone and teleprinter equipment, it housed two generators, while other rooms provided offices, a dining room, and toilets.

As the French network of telephone trunk lines was not available in this remote rural area, new cables had to be laid. By the end of 1942, the 70-kilometre-long stretch between 'Wolfsschlucht 3' and Le Mans, and the 55-kilometre-long stretch between 'Wolfsschlucht 3' and Tours, had been finished, and work was proceeding on the section between 'Wolfsschlucht 3' and Orléans. By the time construction was suspended in August 1943, 'Wolfsschlucht 3' could access the French network at three points and from there connect to the Reich.

Another lighter bunker, eight metres long and five metres wide, was built in the woods north-west of the FHQu to house generators. A sewage farm, discharging into the Loir River, was added to deal with waste water. On top of the hill, four large concrete underground reservoirs were built, in two identical pairs, fed by water pumped from local springs. Total capacity was nearly 500 cubic metres.

One of the best-preserved constructions to be seen today is a large platform, 20 metres long and eight metres wide, standing some two metres above ground. Located near the two main bunkers, it is believed to have been built as a hardstand for six large concrete mixers.

This odd-looking platform, 20 metres long and 8 metres wide, still stands only a few hundred metres from the two large bunkers. Local people say that it was used to accommodate a row of large concrete mixers.

The sewage farm was located at the bottom of the wooded slope, less than 300 metres north-west from the two main bunkers. In 1949 the ditch which ran straight to discharge into the Loir River was still clearly visible. (IGN)

Some 200 metres further along the edge of the wood was a light bunker housing the electric generators. It remained abandoned for decades but the owner, concerned at the danger created by the decaying structure, had it demolished in 2011.

A large number of wooden huts were built all over the site, some in the HQ part of the compound to provide offices, storage, and services and accommodation for the staff. Other hutments were spread out in the various Flak emplacements to serve as barracks for the gun crews. The total number of huts was about 100, which is consistent with the Schmelcher report which recorded the constructions at 'Wolfsschlucht 3' provided 7,000 square metres of useful space.

At Saint-Rimay, a short distance east of the southern entrance of the tunnel, the Flak position at La Cave Brune also comprised the anti-aircraft battery's command post. Although nothing remains to be seen from the air today, the aerial cover from 1949 shows what could then still be seen of the flak positions protecting the headquarters. (IGN and Google)

Being located close to the two large bunkers and the odd platform, the Flak position at la Croix du Bourger was one of the constructions in the 'Wolfsschlucht 3' site that first aroused interest in the 1990s. It comprised a 6.5 by 7-metre-wide platform for an 88mm Flak gun, with a 3.5-metre-wide sloping entrance to bring the gun down into position (top left in the 1949 aerial). In both the left and right-hand side walls, niches about 1.5 metres deep were provided to store ammunition. Beside the emplacement, a 3.2-metre-deep pit, 9 metres wide by 14 metres long, was provided for a 7 by 12-metre hut (bottom right in the aerial). (IGN and Google)

These huts were all of the same type with a central corridor running from one end to the other giving access to rooms on each side. There was a brick chimney for a stove and the walls and roof were insulated with glass wool. The huts were painted grey and were camouflaged under netting.

Each hut was built on a cement base and was surrounded by a concrete wall higher than the hut and banked with earth for blast protection. There was a passageway about one-metre-wide in between the huts and the blast walls.

Numerous anti-aircraft emplacements were to be built on the heights around the site to protect the Führerhauptquartier against air attack: the main ones were at Villavard in the south, Les Roches in the west, Fouassay and Les Bordes in the north, and at Saint-Nicolas, La Cave Brune, Les Grandes Vignes, Croix du Bourger and La Conivardière at Saint-Rimay itself.

Hut platforms on top of the hill above Le Côteau de Fleurigny. At the edge of the wood, the blast walls still survive today, in remarkably good condition. At this one, the protecting walls, which are about 2.2 metres high, provided a platform measuring 7.4 metres by 10.4 metres. Its entrance shows a surprisingly elaborate structure with overhanging porch.

Each hut had a stove with a brick chimney but most of them are now lying broken on the ground. We found this one still standing in the wood.

However, only some had been completed when the whole plan was dropped. On the Flak sites, the huts were generally built in groups of three, some in their own excavation within the blast walls, while sometimes all three huts were installed on the same base.

The German engineers also planned to protect the headquarters with barbed wire and foxholes, but this work had barely started before construction at 'Wolfsschlucht 3' was stopped.

Despite all the work and effort spent on building the complex, it was never used for its intended purpose. From mid-August 1943, the same companies that had built the huts returned to begin carefully dismantling them. Wood frames, windows, and doors, including fixtures and fittings like water pipes and electrical appliances, were all carefully loaded on lorries and taken away. Anything that could not be removed was burned on the spot. All that remained were the concrete foundations and the brick chimneys. All the huts in the Flak emplacements were cleared though those in the central part of the compound were left. It is estimated that over two-thirds of all the huts built were thus removed. German engineers also removed all the telephone cables and lines they had laid down.

Immediately upon receiving news of the Allied landings on the Normandy coast on June 6, 1944, the local OT management team, 'Atlas', took over at 'Wolfsschlucht 3', a possible indication that they had orders to prepare the installation for Hitler's arrival. In the event, the Allies made such substantial territorial gains during the first month that Hitler would not risk placing himself so far west.

The Hist'Orius association organises visits to the Führerhauptquartier. The two large bunkers at the northern entrance of the tunnel are included in the tour, as well as a visit to the interior of the railway tunnel to inspect the armoured doors. The telecommunications bunker is another viewpoint of the tour.

Unlike many of the other Führer headquarters, the Germans did not carry out wholesale demolitions of the site before withdrawing on August 11, simply blowing the power station and setting fire to the telecommunication centre. At around 3 p.m. that same day, three Jeeps from the 22nd Field Artillery Battalion, 4th Armored Division, entered Montoire from the north-west.

The various constructions in the HQ part of the compound were all still intact, including internal furnishings like beds, drawers, desks and crockery, and a visitor just after the German departure described how a small existing manor had been nicely renovated with the oak flooring and the old wooden beams cleaned. Huts were added on each side of the manor house, while more huts were built further down the slope on different levels. The quality of the interior fitting was seen to be impressive. There were large numbers of electric plug sockets, fashionable lighting globes; plenty of wash basins with hot and cold water, toilets and bathrooms, and central heating. The interior was painted in a light cream colour.

Inevitably looting began to remove anything that had been left behind by the Germans, so guards had to be posted to control the compound. With American support, the mayor of Saint-Rimay recovered what he could of the German furniture and artefacts to put them up for auction. The money thus obtained was then distributed to those villagers who had suffered the most from the German occupation activities.

American technicians began to repair the communication network although it is unclear how far the work progressed. Meanwhile, the Americans decided to demolish all the huts still standing, using German POW labour, and have all that remained burned on the spot. The clearance work was finished in October 1944 and by the end of the year the Americans had departed.

The Hist'Orius association now offers a guided tour of 'Wolfsschlucht 3'. Up to date information can be found on their website at **https://www.historius-montoire.fr.**

TWO FHQU NEVER USED, 1944

APPEARING IN SCHMELCHER'S document under numbers 12 and 16, these two FHQu were installed in improbable sites, a Nazi residential complex for one, a fort of the Maginot Line for the other. Neither was used as an FHQu but both had notable post-war use: the Bundesnachrichtendienst, the German foreign intelligence service, was established in 1956 in the premises built for FHQu 'Hagen', and the war command centre for the NATO Central Army Group (CENTAG) was set up in 1961 in the Rochonvillers fort which had been FHQu 'Zigeuner' in 1944.

FHQU 'HAGEN'

Inaugurated in 1938 as part of the grand Nazi plan to make Munich the 'capital of the movement', the 'Reichssiedlung Rudolf Hess' provided for 25 apartment buildings aligned symmetrically around a rectangular plot

Inaugurated in Pullach in 1938, the 'Reichssiedlung' provided for 25 apartment buildings aligned symmetrically around a rectangular plot of land, with a large staff building, the Stabsleiterhaus, in the centre of the estate (top left in this photo).

of land, with a large staff building, the Stabsleiterhaus, in the centre of the estate. Taken over by Bormann, the staff building later became known as Bormann House.

From March 1943, the Organisation Todt began the construction of FHQu 'Hagen', number 12 in the Schmelcher report, in a wooded area adjacent to the 'Reichssiedlung'. It was a project of considerable scale, lasting a year and a half, and requiring 173,750 days of work according to this report. The document reports that the constructions for 'Hagen' were only for the Führerhauptquartier, nothing for the OKH, the OKL or the Reichsführer-SS.

The work mainly involved the construction of a large bunker to the 'Baustärke A' standard, with walls and ceilings of 3.5 metres of reinforced concrete, capable of resisting the heaviest artillery at the time and direct hits from bombs of up to one tonne.

Measuring around 70 metres by 20 metres, the bunker could be sealed off from the outside, with the entrances protected by a pair of gas-proof armoured doors. It provided a little over 800 square metres of usable space in some 30 rooms, a third of which were set up as office spaces. It had its own emergency power supply with diesel engines which were to ensure lighting and operation of the ventilation systems.

In addition, there were four air-raid bunkers, one in the wood east of the main bunker and three in the area of the 'Reichssiedlung' estate, three stone office buildings near the main bunker and a dozen accommodation huts in the wood. Additional accommodation for security teams and drivers, as well as a hut housing the kitchen and dining room, were built at the southern end of the estate, behind Bormann's House. The complex was connected to the railway network, the branch line ending in two sidings for Sonderzüge.

In October 1944, the Führer-Nachrichtenabteilung reported that FHQu 'Siegfried', another code name for the Pullach complex, was only partially equipped with telecommunications facilities and therefore only a small headquarters staff could work in there.

In March 1945, as the Americans approached, the families of the party leaders who resided in the 'Reichssiedlung' left, and the GIs occupied the estate at the end of April. Although it was thoroughly looted, the bunker suffered no damage.

The compound was first used as accommodation for passing troops and as a prison camp, and from the autumn of 1945, for the civil censorship services. In December 1947, the Organisation 'Gehlen' took over.

At the end of the war, General Reinhard Gehlen, who had previously been head of the Fremde Heere Ost department, FHO (Foreign Armies of the East) within the OKH, had placed

No photos of FHQu 'Hagen' under German management have survived to our knowledge and the fact that the BDN, the German foreign intelligence service, has taken up residence on the site makes it impossible to obtain photos today. (Olaf Kosinsky)

Access to the bunker (this photograph) was via a stairwell or elevator at the north corner, and a long corridor of steps served as an emergency exit at the east corner. Entrances were fitted with gas-proof steel doors and a gas sluice, and gas sluices also separated the work and accommodation areas. The concrete structure was enormous: the ground layer was two metres thick, the roof three metres thick, and the outer walls three and a half metres thick. (Olaf Kosinsky)

Accessible by a flight of 20 steps descending from the house, the Bormann house air-raid shelter provided two large rooms each of 20 square metres, four bedrooms each of eight square metres, a telephone exchange, and several smaller rooms. In 2019, Olaf Kosinsky was allowed access to the underground shelter of what is now the Presidential Villa, taking this photo of the bunker corridor. (Olaf Kosinsky)

his organisation and documents at the service of the United States. Financed by the CIA, the organisation collected intelligence on the Red Army and its allies as well as on the situation in the Soviet occupation zone. Initially located in Oberursel in the Taunus, the organisation moved to Pullach in December 1947.

In 1956, West Germany decided to create its own foreign intelligence service, the Bundesnachrichtendienst, BDN, and the Organisation 'Gehlen' soon became part of it. When the Federal Government moved from Bonn to Berlin, the Bundesnachrichtendienst followed and the relocation was completed in 2011. The Pullach facilities now housed the BDN's Technische Aufklärung department.

FHQU 'ZIGEUNER'

Perhaps misled by Allied efforts to instil the idea that the invasion would take place in Pas de Calais, the FHQu planners decided in March 1944 to build a third FHQu in the West, in the east of France, using the underground of a fort of the Maginot Line.

On April 12, Oberbauleiter Müller and Oberstleutnant von Below, Hitler's Luftwaffenadjutant, came by plane from Salzburg to Thionville (Diedenhofen in German) to visit the Rochonvillers fort where work had already started. The galleries were already cleaned, painted, and wired for light.

Rochonvillers was a Gros Ouvrage (major fortress) of the Maginot Line with two artillery blocks armed with 75mm howitzers in turrets, two artillery blocks armed with 135mm mortars in turrets, an artillery block with three 75mm howitzers and a 135mm mortar firing in embrasures, and three infantry blocks armed with machine guns in turrets and embrasures.

With no photos of 'Zigeuner' under German management having been taken to our knowledge, those taken by Signal Corps photographers as American troops reached the Rochonvillers Maginot fort late in 1944 provide a good illustration of what the place must have looked like when the Organisation Todt worked there à few weeks before. Here GIs are about to enter the Rochonvillers munitions entry, note the 60cm rail tracks, the machine-gun embrasure, and the fresh camouflage top of the block. The track ran straight down into the fort and all the way out to the combat blocks, a distance of over two kilometres. (USNA)

Martial Bacquet took this nice comparison at the munitions entrance, with just off to the left the blast wall constructed in front of the entrance in the 1980s as the site was renovated to provide a command centre for the French Army.
(Martial Bacquet, Wikimedia Commons)

Rochonvillers Then and Now. With three 75mm gun embrasures, one 135mm gun embrasure, one light machine-gun cupola and one grenade launcher cupola, Block 5 was the most impressive block of the Rochonvillers fortress. (Morten Jensen)

A machine gun turret — there were three blocks armed with eclipse machine guns turrets – and a GFM cupola – there were 14 in the various blocks of Rochonvillers, including one at each of the personnel and ammunition entries. (Morten Jensen)

At the rear were the two entrance blocks to the fortress, one for personnel, one for ammunition and supplies. The location of these entrances in a ravine allowed a relatively short inclined descent from the ammunition and material entrance to the level of the galleries 30 metres below ground. In 1940 the fortress was garrisoned by some 750 men.

Rochonvillers saw no significant action in May and June 1940, with the Germans largely bypassing the area. On June 30, seven days after the signing of the armistice, the garrison was ordered to evacuate its positions by the French command.

In 1941, the Germans redeveloped the entrance area of the fortress to provide quarters for troops, and pierced a tunnel from the main M1 magazine to the subterranean barrack rooms.

The site was named FHQu 'Zigeuner', but also 'Brunhilde'. When news of the Allied landing in Normandy on June 6 was received, Müller and von Below

This T shaped building of a surface matching the one given in Schmelcher report, still stands near the entrance blocks. It was known for decades as the Führer bunker, but another source indicates it has been built in 1940 by the Luftwaffe. (Morten Jensen)

immediately returned to 'Zigeuner', with two communications officers, to inspect the installation. Work resumed with renewed vigour and at that time, 2,300 workers were employed on the site. From mid-June, Müller remained at 'Zigeuner' to supervise the work and when he left at the end of August, the FHQu was announced as ready for occupancy. The telephone and telex equipment were operational.

Reporting of the construction of 'Zigeuner', Schmelcher indicated that the facilities were intended 'for the FHQu, parts of the OKH, the Reichsführer-SS and the Foreign Minister'. However, his report is vague on what was done, mentioning only 'the extension of three underground works of the Maginot Line' and the construction of wooden huts.

Underground, 15,300 square metres of useable surface were created in the renovated part of the French fort. Above, 1,350 square metres of useable space were provided in wooden huts and 1,080 square metre in concrete-reinforced building. With walls and roof between 50-75cm thick, the entrances and windows fitted with armoured doors and shutters, these buildings offered limited protection, and the Organisation Todt considered them only 'splittersicher', shrapnel proof.

The document drawn up in the autumn of 1944 by the Führer-Nachrichtenabteilung indicates that FHQu 'Brunehilde' was ready for occupation and use as regards to telecommunications facilities. However,

Martial Bacquet ventured down the subterranean fortress with adequate lighting equipment and he took nice photos of the command centre built by the French Army in 1980. Initially, this was the M1 main magazine of the Rochonvillers fortress, then it was part of what the Organisation Todt worked for FHQu 'Hagen' and it became a secret installation, safe from radioactivity and chemical weapons and all but a direct hit with a nuclear weapon. Today unoccupied, access to the site is still prohibited. (Martial Bacquet, Wikimedia Commons)

as Allied armies approached the site, work was abandoned on September 21 and this FHQu was never used for its intended purpose.

In 1961, the war command centre for the NATO Central Army Group (CENTAG) was set up in the main magazine of the fort, with its circulation loop crossed by five galleries. Rochonvillers functioned in this role until 1967 when France withdrew from NATO's integrated command structure and the CENTAG headquarters was then transferred to the Netherlands.

The facility was renovated in 1980 as a command centre for the French Army. The installation was intended to house 500 persons for an extended period, safe from radioactivity and chemical weapons and all but a direct hit with a nuclear weapon. The electrical generating plant was renovated and a new ventilation and filtration system was installed. The concrete faces of the entrance blocks were covered with earth to protect them against blast, and a blast wall was constructed in front of the entrance. From 1981 to 1998, the command centre was maintained by a small number of staff.

Rochonvillers remains under the control of the French army, though no longer occupied, and access to the site is prohibited.

THE ARDENNES OFFENSIVE, 1944, FHQU 'ADLERHORST'

ON OCTOBER 14, 1944, following the hasty retreat of the German armies from France, the Ob. West established his headquarters in the Ziegenberg Castle and the associated bunker complex, the former 'Anlage Mühle' established as FHQu in 1939.

In November, the secret plan for Operation 'Wacht am Rhein', a major counter offensive on the Western Front, designated the Ziegenberg-

In Wiesental, FHQu 'Adlerhorst' established in the seven 'Massivhäuser' built in 1940. Haus I was Hitler's quarters, Haus II was the officers' mess, Haus III housed the OKW and high-level generals, Haus IV was used by generals of the second echelon, Haus V housed the offices of the Ministry of Propaganda, Haus VI was used by Reich ministers and senior Nazi officials, and Haus VII housed Hitler's adjutants, secretaries, and bodyguards.

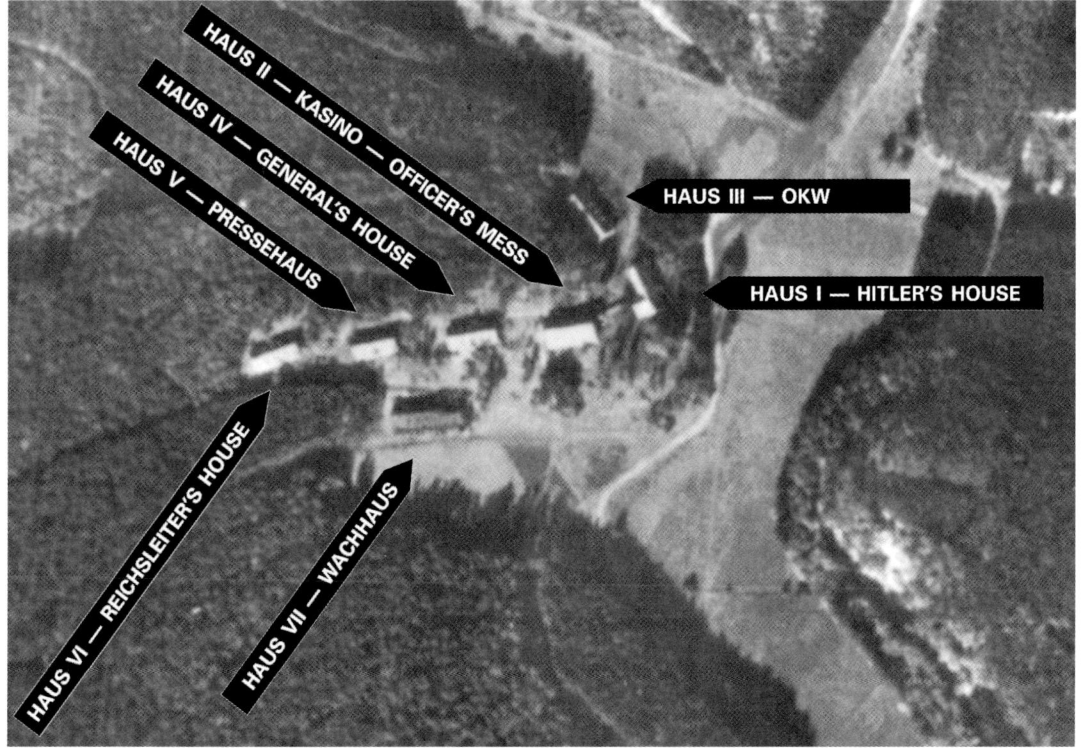

Hitler arrived at FHQu 'Adlerhorst' in the early hours of December 11, 1944. That day and the next day, he received the generals who were to command the troops for the 'Wacht am Rhein' major offensive. This photograph was taken in early January 1945 with (from left to right) Speer, Jodl, Keitel and von Ribbentrop. Speer later recounted how Hitler's 'magnetic gifts' were still working and his optimistic predictions for 1945 transported those present despite the desperate situation. In reality, the end of the Third Reich was four months away.

Wiesental complex as the FHQu for that operation and named it FHQu 'Adlerhorst'. On November 11, Oberbauleiter Müller went to Ziegenberg to prepare the headquarters.

Remarkably, Schmelcher was unaware of this decision when he completed his report that same month, and he described the FHQu 'Mühle' (Ziegenberg) as never having been used as an FHQu, which was true at that date.

The 'Wacht am Rhein' offensive was planned to start on December 16 and Hitler's train (code named 'Brandenburg' since January 1943) left Sonnenwald station late on December 10. It pulled into the Kloster Arnsburg station in the middle of the night and Hitler was then taken by car to the Wiesental compound which then had the cover name 'Amt 600'.

The FHQu was established in the Wiesental compound in the seven 'Massivhäuser' built in 1940. Haus I was Hitler's personal quarters. It consisted of a living room on the ground floor with bedrooms on the first floor while a situation room and a communications centre were set up in the basement. The bunker was connected to Haus II, the officers' mess, by a covered walkway. Haus III housed OKW services and high-level commanders like Göring, Keitel and Jodl, as well as von Rundstedt and Kesselring, who resided there when they were at 'Adlerhorst'.

Haus IV was used by the second echelon generals, like Guderian and von Manteuffel. Services of the Propaganda Ministry occupied Haus V, while Reich ministers and senior Nazi officials used Haus VI.

Haus VII was the largest of the seven 'Massivhäuser'. Named the

'Wachhaus', it housed Hitler's adjutants, secretaries, and maintenance staff, as well as his bodyguards. The whole complex was guarded, and a network of anti-aircraft batteries was set up around the surrounding hills.

On December 11 and 12, Hitler received in two groups the generals commanding the corps and divisions that were to launch the offensive. The generals were driven to the 'Adlerhorst' in a bus on a long, circuitous route through the mountains to deliberately confuse them about the location of the FHQu. Hitler ended his speech with the exhortation 'The enemy must be smashed, now or never! Long Live Germany!'

Hitler's daily routine was to wake up at midday, and he then read the latest reports and received the first callers. He had dinner at 2 p.m. with his secretaries, Christa Schroeder and Gerda Christian. The daily situation conference took place at 4 p.m., attenders being Göring, Keitel, Jodl, von Rundstedt, and Himmler, and the reporting officers. Hitler dined, with his two secretaries, at 8 p.m. and went to bed between 3 and 5 a.m.

'Wacht am Rhein', better known to the Western Allies as the 'Battle of the Bulge' or the 'von Rundstedt Offensive', began at 5.30 a.m. on December 16, 1944. While Hitler and the OKW were at FHQu 'Adlerhorst', the OKH continued to oversee the Eastern Front from the Zossen headquarters. The head of the Generalstabes des Heeres, Generaloberst Heinz Guderian, therefore had to shuttle between Berlin and Ziegenberg to confer with Hitler. He first came on December 24, to warn Hitler of the threat of a Soviet breakthrough in north-west Hungary. He pressed for the transfer of forces to the Eastern Front to confront the attack but Hitler accepted almost nothing.

At the situation conference on December 26, when the offensive was already running out of steam, far from having achieved its objectives, Göring privately suggested to Hitler that it might be time to negotiate an armistice. Hitler became very angry and threatened to court-martial him.

On December 31, he made a radio broadcast to the German people from the 'Pressehaus' before going to Haus I to celebrate the New Year with his close associates and his secretaries. Speer, who had just arrived, later described the scene: 'Adjutants, doctors, secretaries, Bormann, the whole circle except for the generals attached to the Führer's headquarters, were gathered around Hitler drinking champagne. The alcohol had relaxed everyone, but the atmosphere was still subdued. Hitler seemed to be the only one in the company who was drunk without having taken any stimulating beverage. He was in the grip of a permanent euphoria. Hitler made optimistic forecasts for 1945. The present low point would soon be overcome, he said; in the end we would be victorious. The circle took these prophecies in silence. Only Bormann enthusiastically seconded him. After more than two hours, during which Hitler spread around his credulous optimism, his followers, including myself, were transported despite all their scepticism into a more sanguine state. His magnetic gifts were still operative.' Guderian returned on January 9 to press again for the transfer of forces to the East before it was too late, but Hitler angrily refused.

On March 19, as the headquarters of Ob. West was established in the former FHQu, three squadrons of Thunderbolt fighter-bombers attacked the Ziegenberg Castle, causing heavy damage to the castle and surrounding buildings.

The Americans reached the FHQu on March 30, here a jeep passes the security barrier on the road from Ziegenberg. They found Haus I and many other buildings destroyed, but the 'Pressehaus' (Haus V) and the 'Wachhaus' (Haus VII) had escaped demolition. In 1974, *After the Battle* visited the site of FHQu 'Adlerhorst' and took this comparison where the barrier once stood.

Heavily camouflaged among the trees, this is how the 'Wachhaus' appeared to the American soldier when they arrived in Wiesental. Haus VII is the only one of the seven 'Massivhäuser' built in Wiesental that remains recognisable today.

Hitler left FHQu 'Adlerhorst' on the evening of January 15 for the Hungen station where his train was parked. He was back at the Reichskanzlei in Berlin at 10 a.m. the next morning. His one-month stay at FHQu 'Adlerhorst' was his last stay outside Berlin. On March 9, Generalfeldmarschall Albert Kesselring

Extensive camouflaging made Haus III, the OKW headquarters building, almost impossible to detect. Note the sunken guard post roofed with logs.

This is how Haus I, Hitler's quarters, appeared when the GIs reached Wiesental. A villa stands today on this same site, partly where was the bunker.

succeeded to von Rundstedt as Ob. West and he moved to Ziegenberg with his staff the next night.

On March 19, alerted to the compound's original destination and unsure whether Hitler was there, the Allies sent three squadrons of Thunderbolt fighter-bombers to attack the castle. The three-wave raid, which lasted 45 minutes, caused heavy damage to the castle and surrounding buildings.

On March 28, as American leaders approached, Kesselring and his staff evacuated Ziegenberg after ordering the destruction of the complex. The Americans reached the compound on March 30 and found Haus I and many other buildings reduced to burned shells, but the 'Pressehaus' (Haus V), and the 'Wachhaus' (Haus VII), had escaped demolition.

Today, the castles of Ziegenberg and Kransberg are in private hands and are not accessible to the public. The Wiesental complex is largely intact, but the bunkers are mostly private sites and not accessible to the public.

THE CAPTURE OF THE BERGHOF, 1945

IN THE SPRING OF 1943, the Allies' conquest of North Africa and their advance into Italy made the threat of air raids against Obersalzberg possible and the site's anti-aircraft defences were strengthened, to include 60 Flak guns positioned on favourable heights.

Construction of air-raid bunkers began this summer. A first system of galleries was built to serve the Berghof, another for the Bormann house, and more for the Göring house, the men of the SS barracks, the guests of the Platterhof.

Most of the galleries were round-arched, measuring 2.5 metres high and 1.75 metres wide. To the right and left of the galleries, spaces were dug out to provide usable spaces. These rooms were up to 15 metres long, 2.8 metres high at the highest point and 3.5 metres wide. From the houses and buildings, steps led down about 40 metres to the galleries. As Hitler began to experience difficulty climbing stairs during his stay in the summer of 1944,

Construction of underground air-raid shelters deep in the rock at the Obersalzberg began in 1943. Galleries were built to serve the various houses and buildings, steps descending about 40 metres to the galleries. By the end of the war, more than four kilometres of galleries had been dug, providing 75 rooms, or nearly 4,000 square metres of usable space. This plan appears in a document published in 1964 by the US Berchtesgaden Recreation Area, engineer section.

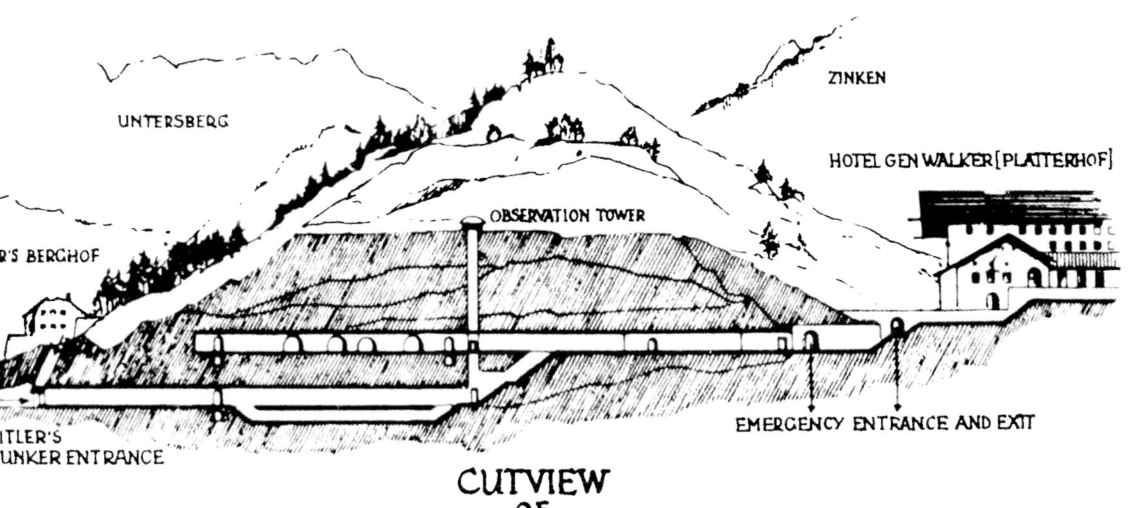

Having served as a communications centre and quarters for security units in the Nazi era, the Hotel 'zum Türken' was severely damaged in the bombing raid of April 1945. After the war, the Schuster family, the pre-Nazi period owner, was able to get the hotel back and restore it. The hotel's guest can have a look at the galleries under the hotel, and post cards were published, like this one in the 1960s: 'Hitler bunker in Hotel Türken, stairs to the machine gun stands'.

work began to install an elevator from the Berghof to the air-raid bunker, but it was never completed. Each gallery system had an escape tunnel to the outside, with steel doors.

By the end of the war, more than four kilometres of galleries had been dug into the rock, two kilometres of which contained 75 rooms, or nearly 4,000 square metres of usable space.

Stricter security measures were put in place in September 1943 and a new Sperrkreis A was created at Obersalzberg: no one could enter Sperrkreis A without a valid pass, no car could enter Sperrkreis A, except for the cars of the Reichsministers, the Reichsleiters and the field marshals. Even these high-ranking personalities, as well as anybody accompanying them, had to be in possession of a pass and present it whenever requested.

In the spring of 1944, Hitler left the Berghof after his final stay, and Bormann ordered that a new, deeper system of galleries be dug into the mountain at least 100 metres underground. However, due to lack of construction materials, work did not progress much.

In mid-1944, the construction of a new FHQu in a central location was considered, and Obersalzberg appeared to be a perfect location.

The Organisation Todt sent a management team, named 'Lothar', to Berchtesgaden to build the new FHQu.

The first air attack on Berchtesgaden was on February 20, 1945, when eight P-47 fighter bombers from the Fifteenth Air Force could not complete their mission in Italy and attacked the Berchtesgaden sector instead. This striking photo was taken at a later date, after the capture of the Berghof. (USNA)

In his report from November 1944, Schmelcher mentions that FHQu under construction at Berchtesgaden comprised two parts: in Strub for the FHQu and the OKH, and in Winkl and Reichenhall for the OKH. The report states that the work was planned to take place from October 1944 to the end of March 1945. The work was to take a total of 56,000 working days.

The work will provide 2,800 square metres of usable space in tunnels, 2,090 in bunkers, and 18,000 in others buildings. It was planned to use 43,000 cubic metres of concrete.

In the autumn of 1944, the Führer-Nachrichtenabteilung reported Berchtesgaden as one of the four FHQu that were ready for occupation and use as regards to their telecommunications facilities. (The others were 'Wolfschanze' in East Prussia, 'Felsennest', then known as 'WO' in Rodert, and 'Zigeuner' near Thionville.) In his report from November 1944, Schmelcher mentions that the installation consisted of two parts: in Strub (called Franken-Strub, a code name?) for the FHQu and the OKH, and in Winkl and Reichenhall for the OKH. The report states that the work took place from

This reconnaissance aerial photo taken before the attack on April 25, 1945, shows all the principal buildings on Obersalzberg: in the centre, the Platterhof garage and servants' quarters, and the SS barracks, training hall and garages (the square construction); immediately above them, the Berghof and the offices of the Security Service (formerly 'Gasthaus zum Türken'); top right, Bormann's house and Göring's house (partly out of the photo); bottom, the Platterhof Pension.

October 1944 to the end of March 1945 and included the construction of a large bunker in Strub, as well as a tunnel and wooden huts in Winkl.

Keitel and Jodl were in favour of moving the FHQu to Berchtesgaden but Hitler was apparently reluctant. He authorised the construction of another FHQu facility in Thuringia, possibly in Ohrdruf, at the Truppenübungsplatz (military training ground), but the lack of documents left the question unresolved. In his report of November 1944, Schmelcher made no mention of this installation in Ohrdruf.

On April 19, 1945, coming from Zossen, groups of the WFSt settled in Strub and General August Winter, Jodl's deputy, arrived on the 24th. That day, he was appointed Chef Führungsstab Süd (Command Staff South).

Göring sent a telex to Berlin in which, on the grounds that Hitler was encircled there and therefore no longer able to direct affairs, he arrogated to himself the succession of the Führer. Hitler considered this an act of treason and ordered Göring's arrest. At 5 p.m. on the 24th, Göring was placed under house arrest in his Obersalzberg house.

On April 25, Bomber Command launched a massive raid against

The Bomber Command launched a massive raid against the Obersalzberg on April 25. The force comprised 359 Lancasters from No. 1 and 5 Groups and 16 Mosquitos from No. 8 Group whose role was to guide the bombers to the target. The alert was sounded on Obersalzberg at 9.30 a.m. This photo was taken when a bomb just exploded a few ten metres north of the Berghof.

Obersalzberg. The alert was sounded at 9.30 a.m. and when the attack began half an hour later all workers and residents were safe in the air raid shelters. The bombers had difficulty identifying their targets because the snow covering the ground blended in with the low clouds. The bombing lasted an hour and a total of 1,230 tonnes of bombs were dropped. One side of the Berghof was destroyed, the Goring and Bormann houses were seriously damaged, as were the SS barracks and the Platterhof, and the entire area was heavily cratered. The loss of life was light, only six people killed out of the 3,500 sheltering in the rock tunnels.

The only highly-ranking personalities at Obersalzberg at the time of the

Leading elements of the 1st Battalion, 7th Infantry Regiment, moved into Berchtesgaden at 3.58 p.m. on May 4. Having just passed through Stanggass, this Sherman of the 756th Tank Battalion — attached to the 3rd Infantry Division — was pictured as it reached Berchtesgaden. In 2010, veteran of the division placed an historic marker on this spot. (USNA)

attack, Göring survived the bombing and he was then taken with his family to Austria by the SS.

After informing the civilian authorities in Berchtesgaden that he did not intend to defend the area, the SS commander withdrew his troops southward. The building projects team followed, leaving behind a huge debt to construction firms and workers.

On the Obersalzberg, the situation was chaotic; with the tunnels and buildings unguarded, people began looting the food, clothing and goods stored there. Some form of order was restored by Herr Georg Grethlein, head of the largest construction firm on the mountain, with the help of some of his four hundred-odd employees. (He was mistakenly shot by American soldiers and killed, as was his driver, later that day.)

On Friday, May 4, those SS troops left poured petrol into the Berghof and set it on fire.

The capture of Berchtesgaden was assigned to the 101st Airborne Division, XXI Corps, and the 506th Parachute Infantry Regiment started early on May 4. The leaders crossed the Inn River near Rosenheim, skirted the Chiemsee, but were stopped at a blown bridge near Inzell. The points of the French 2ème Division Blindée, which also had orders to take Berchtesgaden, were already blocked there. The 506th began building a Bailey bridge but from the far side of the stream Germans started laying machine gun fire at the

Riding on an M36 tank destroyer of the 601st Tank Destroyer Battalion, GIs of the 3rd Infantry Division reached the palace square in Berchtesgaden. The WWI memorial painting by Munich artist Josef Hengge now includes the dates for World War II, 1914-1918 left of the cross, 1939-1945 right of it. (USNA)

There just were not enough roads that day; a message received by XXI Corps offered the explanation: 'Everybody and his brother are trying to get into the town'. When a French column arrived at the Saalach bridge, the GIs guarding the bridge stopped them and Général Leclerc went to see Major-General O'Daniel (this photo). It was only some time after he had learned of the capture of Berchtesgaden by the 7th Infantry that O'Daniel did allow the French column to pass the bridge.

bridge builders. The paratroopers had to cross the stream, and climb the hill to chase away the German defenders.

Just to the east, in the XV Corps sector, the 3rd Infantry Division was already in possession of much of Salzburg. When he learnt that neither the 101st Airborne Division nor the 2ème Division Blindée had yet reached the Saalach River, the 3rd Infantry Division commander, Major-General John W. O'Daniel, took matters into his own hands. In possession of two bridges over the Saalach River, his 7th Infantry Regiment was in the most favourable position to swoop down on Berchtesgaden. O'Daniel decided to send the regiment out of the division zone, to steal the coveted town from the American paratroopers and French armoured forces.

The regiment commander, Colonel John A. Heintges, quickly issued the orders to push the 1st and 3rd Battalions over the Saalach bridges. While the foot troops and light vehicles crossed on a small wooden bridge, engineers cleared a railway bridge to allow passage of the artillery and attached armour and tank-destroyers. O'Daniel ordered that guards be placed on the two bridges and that they let no one to pass over them except 7th Infantry personnel and vehicles.

At 9.30 a.m. the 1st Battalion seized Bad Reichenhall, while the 3rd Battalion captured Marzoll. The SS commander having withdrawn his troops southward after making clear that he had no intention of defending the area, Landrat Theodor Jacob disbanded the local Volkssturm and headed north from Berchtesgaden that afternoon. Near Winkl, he met with the leaders of the 7th Infantry Regiment and discussed surrender with Lieutenant Colonel Kenneth Wallace, commanding officer of the 1st Battalion.

The 1st Battalion entered Berchtesgaden at 3.58 p.m., without a fight, and 2,000 German soldiers surrendered. Moving the longer route around from Marzoll to Schellenberg the 3rd Battalion entered Berchtesgaden from the north-east at 4.30 p.m. Units of the 2ème Division Blindée took the Obersalzberg at 6 p.m.

With the capture of the Obersalzberg, a Nazi holy place, this is the end of this first book in our history of the FHQu. Our second volume will deal with the Führerhauptquartiere in the East, and will end at the Führerbunker in Berlin, with the final days of the Third Reich.

O'Daniel also lifted the ban for the 101st Parachute Division, and two battalions of the 506th Parachute Infantry Regiment followed the 7th Regiment's route and reached Berchtesgaden in the morning of May 5. The 3rd Battalion finished to repair the bridge and moved on to Berchtesgaden by the regiment's original route and arrived in the afternoon. Having just passed in front of the church, these soldiers moved south along the then Adolf-Hitler-Strasse, now Maximilian Strasse. (USNA and Eduardo Balar)

The Berghof was still smouldering on May 5 after being set on fire by SS troops when this photo was taken, one of the first photos taken of the Berghof after its capture. Note the remaining snow from a light snowfall the night before.
(USNA)

This is how the men of the 7th Infantry Regiment found the Berghof on May 5. At the top of the hill we see the ruins of Bormann's house. Contrary to what appears in many books today, *Band of Brothers* for example, the 101st Airborne Division was not the first Allied troop to reach Berchtesgaden or the Obersalzberg. It is possible that a few vehicles from the French 2ème Division Blindée were actually the first Allied soldiers to reach Berchtesgaden, and perhaps the Obersalzberg, but they did not stop and drove on. (USNA)

Another of the very first photos of the ruined Berghof, this one taken by Paul Gloaguen, soldier of the 2ème Division Blindée, therefore one of the first visitors of the captured Obersalzberg. In the foreground we see the Gasthaus zum Türken, communications centre and quarters for security units. Note, uphill on the left, the large craters left by the Bomber Command bombs on April 25, 1945. (Paul Gloaguen)

Soldiers of the 7th Infantry Regiment relax at the foot of the staircase to the first floor on chairs taken from the terrace. Others enjoy the view from the terrace. Original caption identifies them as (L-R) Private Vincent Constable, Private Joseph Bryan, Corporal Donald Shumaker and Corporal Frank Goodney. (USNA)

On May 6, the 7th Infantry Regiment was ordered to withdraw and assemble at Salzburg, its rightful area, and Berchtesgaden was handed over to the 101st Airborne Division and French troops. The Berghof became a major attraction and, as the 101st Airborne Division's story, *Rendezvous with Destiny,* recounts, visitors came 'in trucks, weapons-carriers, jeeps, motor-cycles, sedans, ambulances. By the first of June they were averaging three thousand daily and as many as ten thousand on Sundays.' (USHHM)

The famed window blown open by the bombing, Japanese-American soldiers with the 522nd Field Artillery Battalion enjoy an uncluttered view of Untersberg and Berchtesgaden.
(USNA and USHHM)

Soldiers of the 101st Airborne Division climbed up to the Eagle's Nest to relax in the original furnishings. This photograph was taken very early after the capture of the Obersalzberg, on May 5 or 6, for the place is still intact: the chairs and tables, the carpets, even a vase were still untouched. The same room is open today as a restaurant during the summer months.
(USNA and Itto Ogami, Wikimedia Commons)

Sonnenterasse, Then and Now. GIs relaxes in the sun on the south-facing terrace. The right door gives access to the then kitchen, further along the right wall were the two windows of Hitler's study, then the four windows of the dining room.
(USNA and Itto Ogami, Wikimedia Commons)

Rendezvous with Destiny: 'The airborne troops acted as guides and guards and signs warned against taking souvenirs in Hitler's houses, but everything removable, from bed springs to doorknobs and light fixtures, went.' Within weeks, the souvenir hunters had virtually emptied the Berghof of anything that could be taken. The conference room was already thoroughly looted when these two GIs examine the fireplace. (USNA)

In 1951, the American occupying forces agreed to the reopening of Obersalzberg on the condition that the ruins of the Berghof and the Göring and Bormann houses were removed. Protests followed the decision, with attacks in the press, but the German government, as well as American authorities, were adamant that political protests could only be avoided by removing the ruins. The Berghof was dynamited by a German demolition firm at 5.05 p.m. on April 30, 1952.

The Göring and Bormann houses were also demolished, the ruins of the SS barracks next to the Platterhof were cleared, but the Platterhof Hotel escaped destruction. Purchased in 1937 by Bormann for the Party, the original building was demolished and a new building was constructed on site. Any German who pilgrimaged to the Obersalzberg to see the Führer could stay a night at the new Platterhof Hotel for only RM 1. In 1943, the necessities of war turned the hotel into a military hospital. The hotel was expropriated by the Americans in 1945, and thus escaped destruction in 1952. Rebuilt and renovated as the General Walker Hotel, it became a recreation centre for US Military personnel.

This is the ruined Platterhof garage as it appeared in 1984: this large multi-story garage building provided accommodation on the upper floors for hotel staff. The complex was returned to the German government in 1995 and it was demolished, along with the ruins of the garage, in 2000. The site was transformed into a parking lot for the Dokumentation Obersalzberg centre and the Kehlsteinhaus bus ticket office.

A very small part of the network of underground shelters is accessible, here the entrance to the Platterhof bunker, see plan page 165.
(Cor2701, Wikimedia Commons)

Another entrance to the underground galleries system, here near the Hotel zum Türken.

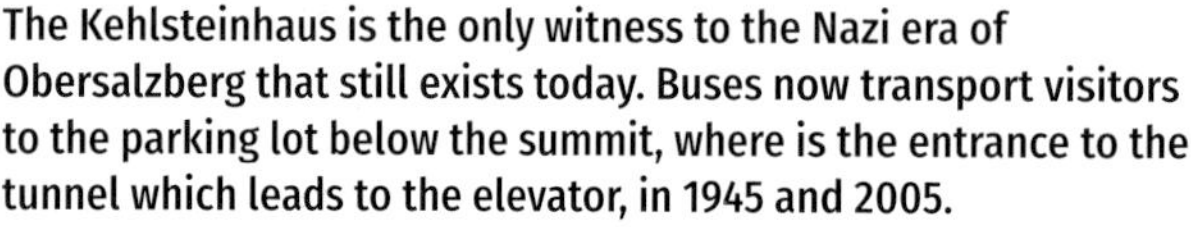

The Kehlsteinhaus is the only witness to the Nazi era of Obersalzberg that still exists today. Buses now transport visitors to the parking lot below the summit, where is the entrance to the tunnel which leads to the elevator, in 1945 and 2005.
(Thérèse Bonney and Frans Banja Mulder, Wikimedia Commons)

The entrance tunnel. At the end of the tunnel, in a circular waiting room, a pair of bronze doors provide entry to the elevator. It takes visitors up to the Kehlsteinhaus, 124 metres higher.
(Geolina, Wikimedia Commons)

FHQU THEN AND NOW IN COLOUR

Hitler had ties to the Obersalzberg since the mid-1920s, having sought refuge here after his release from prison following his unsuccessful attempt to seize power in Munich in 1923, and after he was sworn in as chancellor in 1933, the Berghof became a centrepiece of Nazi propaganda. Stories portrayed him as a man of culture, dog lover, and good neighbour, and, based on these propaganda sources, William George Fitz-Gerald, writing for the British magazine *Homes & Gardens*, described Hitler as 'his own decorator, designer, and furnisher, as well as architect', and the chalet as 'bright and airy'.

OBERSALZBERG

The Berghof became an attraction in the mid-1930s, and every day hundreds of admirers paraded past the house, hoping to catch a glimpse of the Führer, like this group of traditionally dressed farmers and their wives in June 1937. Taken from the road below the Hotel 'zum Türken', this photo shows two tracks leading to the hill where the Berghof once stood. The main drive to the Berghof was the one further down the hill. (David Holt, Wikimedia Commons)

Countless photos were taken on the stairway leading up to the front door of the Berghof. Official photos, but also less formal photos, like this one where a group of BDM girls posed for a souvenir photo with Hitler in 1938. The Bund Deutscher Mädel (BDM, League of German Young Girls) was the women's wing of the Nazi Party's youth movement, the Hitler Youth. The retaining wall cut into the hillside is all that remains today of the Berghof, in the woods that have grown up all around the hillside.
(ATB/USNA and Peter Emile, Wikimedia Commons)

A security perimeter, called the 'Führer Area', was established around the Berghof and gates controlled access. This elaborate road-spanning gatehouse controlled the road just below the Berghof (seen at the top right). The wooden structure has disappeared, but the stone foundations are still visible today at the side of the road.
(SSETO and Cor2701, Wikimedia Commons)

After the Duke and Duchess of Windsor visited Hitler at the Berghof on October 22, 1937, Robert Ley, leader of the Deutsche Arbeitsfront (German Labour Front), accompanied the Duke and Duchess to Berchesgaden station. Ley's alcoholism was noted during the visit, and at one point he crashed their car into a gate.
(Peter Plenk and Geolina, Wikimedia Commons)

The Kehlsteinhaus is the only witness to the Nazi era of Obersalzberg that still exists today. The structure of the building was made of concrete, with the exterior clad in granite blocks and the interior of the reception hall clad in sandstone blocks. This period view shows the large rug covering the centre of the room, as well as the tapestry above the fireplace.

Hitler and Goebbels in front of the fireplace of the Kehlsteinhaus in 1938, on the left is Helga, six years old, Goebbels' daughter. The same fireplace in 2012, pictured from the opposite angle. In May 1945, it took less than a week for souvenir hunters to strip the Berghof of everything of interest, and the most desperate among them then began chipping off pieces of marble from the fireplace. (Itto Ogami, Wikimedia Commons)

FÜHRERSONDERZUG

Hitler's pre-war Sonderzug had ten coaches of uniform size, painted dark green and drawn by two locomotives. At the outbreak of war two anti-aircraft wagons were added, one behind the locomotive and another at the rear, each armed with two 20mm guns and manned by a crew of 20 to 30 gunners.

On September 12, 1939, while the Führersonderzug was parked on a siding at Illnau, Silesia, von Ribbentrop and Hitler strolled alongside the train to stretch their legs. The same railway station as it appears today, now Jelowa in Poland. (ATB/USNA and Historical sites)

'FELSENNEST'

Hitler arrived at FHQu 'Felsennest' early in the morning of May 10, just as the Wehrmacht was attacking in the West after eight months of 'Drôle de Guerre'. This photo was taken a few days later with Oberst Rudolf Schmundt, Heeres Adjutant, and Major Gerhard Engel, OKH Adjutant. (ATB/USNA)

The FHQu installations on the 'Felsennest' hill were destroyed by German engineers at the beginning of March 1945. Bushes and trees have now invaded the site, these are the ruins of a bunker photographed by Adri Kramer in 2019. (Adri Kramer)

The concrete foundations on which the prefabricated huts were built still stand in the woods. (Hans-Günther and Jürgen Morr)

'WOLFSSCHLUCHT'

Work on the construction of FHQu 'Wolfsschlucht' at Brûly-de-Pesche started on May 25, and Hitler arrived on June 6. An elaborate signpost has been erected in the centre of the village, although it does not appear to have been completed at the time this photo was taken. Only the arrow pointing towards the Luftschutzraum (air raid shelter) was then in place. (ATB and Google)

The works included removing the church spire to install a water tank. At the end of June, after the departure of the FHQu, the Organisation Todt rebuilt the spire before leaving. (ATB and Google)

Hitler and Bormann examine a batch of photographs in the street de Brûly-de-Pesche. Remarkably, the village has remained absolutely the same for over eight decades and even the school latrines in the background remain unchanged!

Being billed as 'Hitler's Bunker', the bunker lay hidden in the dense wood for decades immediately north of the village and appeared on many local postcards.

The trees surrounding the bunker have long been preserved as they were during the FHQu era, including white markings painted to mark them at night. (Louis Baijot, Wikimedia Commons)

Two wooden huts were rebuilt in the early 1990s on the sites where Hitler's hut and the officers' mess were located, and 'Brûly-de-Pesche 1940' now manages tours of the former FHQu. The site today is in much less dense forest than it was in 1940 because in 2019 a storm damaged many trees in the forest and they had to be felled. (Stefan Kühn, Wikimedia Commons)

'TANNENBERG'

Goebbels came to the FHQu 'Tannenberg' to discuss with Hitler about his return to Berlin after the stunning victory against France. He discussed here with Himmler and SS-Obersturmführer Gunter d'Alquen in front of the camouflaged bunker. Note the steel shutters flanking the windows and doors. Gunter d'Alquen was chief editor of the weekly Das Schwarze Korps, the official newspaper of the SS. (ATB/USNA

Foundations on which the prefabricated huts were built, and concrete remains still stand on the hill where FHQu 'Tannenberg' once stood. (Ulrich Classen and Wstenschke, Wikimedia Commons)

'FRÜHLINGSSTURM'

The Führersonderzug arrived in Mönichkirchen, Austria, at 7.20 a.m. on April 12, 1941, to serve as Führerhauptquartier 'Frühlingssturm' during the campaign in the Balkans. This picture was taken on the morning of April 13, 1941, when Generaloberst von Brauchitsch, Army C-in-C, to attend a conference. What was the fate of the Führersonderzug? Hitler used it for the last time when, with 'Wacht am Rhein' having miscarried, he left FHQu 'Adlerhorst' on January 15, 1945 and returned to Berlin the next morning. Except for a short visit by motorised column to the Oder front on March 11, he never again left the Reichskanzlei and the Führerbunker deep under its garden. Their role as the last Führerhauptquartier remains to be described in the second book of this series. The Führersonderzug was moved in the early spring of 1945 from its Berlin-Tempelhof siding to Bruck, south of Zell-am-See. At the end of April, on Hitler's personal orders, the Führerwagen (Sal4ü-37, number 10 206 Bln) was removed from the Führersonderzug and destroyed near Mallnitz on May 7, 1945. The aim was to prevent the Allies from exposing the vehicle. Later in May, GIs discovered the former Führersonderzug parked on a siding in Pullach. What remained of the various Sonderzüge was used by Britain and the United States in occupied post-war Germany, before being returned to the new German Railways Authority in the 1950s. The various cars were separated and used separately during the 1960s and 1970s until the last car in operation was reportedly scrapped in June 1973. The Mönichkirchen station was closed in 1996 and the abandoned building was classified as a historic monument. This photo of 2016 shows how the building has remained unchanged for eight decades, even the wooden extension on the side is still standing. (ATB/USNA and Priwo)

'WOLFSSCHLUCHT 2'

At Margival, near Soissons in France, the huge FHQu 'Wolfsschlucht 2' contained seven heavy bunkers of 'Baustärke A' standard and 13 light bunkers. This is how Bau 1, the Führerbunker where Hitler only came once on June 17, 1944, appeared when the GIs reached 'Wolfsschlucht 2' on the afternoon of August 29. This photo was taken by men of the 602nd Engineer Battalion who inspected the abandoned German headquarters soon after its capture. (USNA)

The 'ASW2' association has worked hard for two decades to clean and secure the former 'Wolfsschlucht 2', and they now manage visits of the site. These start at the southern entrance of the camp located at the village of Margival, and visitors are first taken along a series of large bunkers, Bau 18 through to Bau 9. Then, having reached the former FHQu railway station, one is taken to the northern sector, with stops at Bau 5 and Bau 8, and then at the Führerbunker. (Bruno Renoult)

Without the Teehaus that appears in the top left corner, it would have been difficult to identify this particular bunker for they were all built along the same general lines. It is in fact the western end of Bau 5, the huge bunker housing the complex's telephone exchange. (USNA and ATB)

'WOLFSSCHLUCHT 3'

At Saint-Rimay, near Vendôme in France, FHQu 'Wolfsschlucht 3' comprised two heavy bunkers of 'Baustärke A' standard and numerous wooden huts, with additional accommodation for Flak and security forces throughout. Taken on August 11, 1944, shortly after the Germans left and American troops arrived, this photo of the 'Führerbunker' shows the camouflage netting still in place. This photo also shows how close the bunker was to the tunnel entrance, the railway line passing through a cutting in between the bunker and the house in the background. The bunker was cleared of trees and bushes in 2017, giving Jean Paul Brillard the opportunity to take this comparison for us. (Jean Paul Brillard)

Taken in September 1944, this photo shows the long wooden platform built alongside the track to allow for easier unloading of both the labour force and the construction materials, and for the benefit of Hitler's entourage alighting there once the construction was completed. On the hillside beyond, above the second 'Baustärke A' bunker, the Germans added huts on each side of an existing small manor house to provide additional office space.

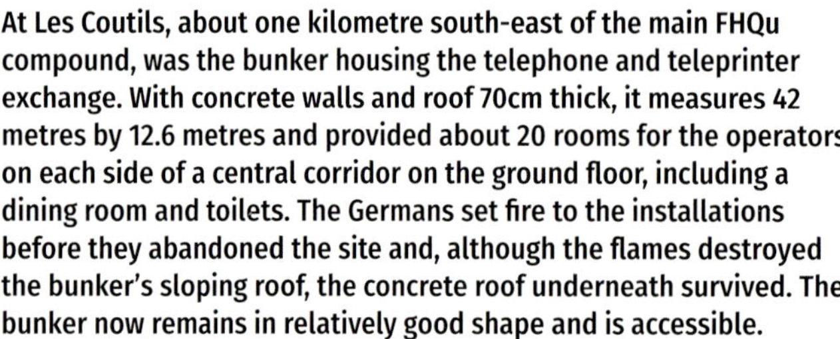

At Les Coutils, about one kilometre south-east of the main FHQu compound, was the bunker housing the telephone and teleprinter exchange. With concrete walls and roof 70cm thick, it measures 42 metres by 12.6 metres and provided about 20 rooms for the operators on each side of a central corridor on the ground floor, including a dining room and toilets. The Germans set fire to the installations before they abandoned the site and, although the flames destroyed the bunker's sloping roof, the concrete roof underneath survived. The bunker now remains in relatively good shape and is accessible.

'ADLERHORST'

In December 1944, FHQu 'Adlerhorst' established in the seven 'Massivhäuser' built in 1940 as part of 'Anlage Wiesental' and Hitler arrived on the 11th. His one-month stay at FHQu 'Adlerhorst' was his last stay outside Berlin. Ob. West, the Commander-in-Chief West, established headquarters at the FHQu in early March 1945. At the end of the month, as the Americans approached, they evacuated and engineers destroyed the complex. In 1956, students from the American High School in Frankfurt inspected the ruins of the main bunker in Wiesental. (Neil P. Albaugh)

Since then, the remains of the blown up 'Massivhäuser' have been cleared and many new houses have been built over the site. The 'Wachhaus' (Haus VII), had escaped demolition and a new house now occupies the same spot. In 1957, Gatshof Adlerhorst established on the site of Haus III, the OKW headquarters building, and a villa is now situated on the site of Haus 1, Hitler's quarters. See page 159 for an aerial photo of FHQu 'Adlerhorst' in 1945.

According to Schmelcher, most of the works were done for the FHQu, with only small works at the Kransberg Castle to provide 2,600 square metres for the services of the Reichsführer-SS. The bunker at the Kransberg Castle as it appears in 2011. (Tadam, Wikimedia Commons)

Just below Ziegenberg Castle, on the side of the road to Wiesental, this air raid shelter still exists today. (Tadam, Wikimedia Commons)

OBERSALZBERG CAPTURED

The agitation and looting at the Berghof were such in May and June 1945 that to restore order, a guard post was set up at the entrance to the drive way. Tacked onto the Bormann Tree, a sign reads 'Eintritt Für Zivil verboten', entry for civilians forbidden. (Thérèse Bonney, The Bancroft Library, University of California, Berkeley)

The Gasthaus zum Türken, the communications centre and quarters for the Reichssicherheitsdienst, the security men patrolling the Berghof, escaped destruction in 1952. After the war, the ruined building was purchased back by the family who owned it before the Nazi era and after its reconstruction it opened as Hotel 'zum Türken'.
(USNA and FST)

When *After the Battle* visited the Obersalzberg in 1974, the Berghof's garage, the roof of which formed the terrace of the house, was intact. The drive, up which so many famous personalities ascended, still remained. The garage was demolished in the late 1990s, the official reason was that the underground ruin posed a security risk, but just as important was the desire to prevent it from becoming a pilgrimage site for neo-Nazis.

Rubble was dumped on the site in 1952 and again during the destruction of the remaining buildings in the early 2000s and in consequence, the current ground level on most of the Berghof site is higher than the level of origin. In the woods that have grown up all around the hill the retaining wall cut into the hillside is all that remains today of the Berghof.
(Peter Emile, Wikimedia Commons)

Hitler's guest house was another important building still standing in 1974 and it was featured on the cover of *After the Battle*. The building was demolished in 1997 to allow the construction on the site of a documentation centre which opened its doors in 1999. Managed by the Institut für Zeitgeschichte (Institute for Contemporary History) of Munich, the Dokumentation Obersalzberg centre extends over two floors of the new building and part of the network of underground shelters is accessible.

The Kehlsteinhaus Then and Now. In May 1945, a group from the 522nd Field Artillery Battalion climbed up to the Eagle's Nest. In the early 1950s, the US authorities intended to demolish the Eagle's Nest as well as the other ruins of Obersalzberg but the Landrat of Berchtesgaden, Theodor Jacob, made a strong protest against the proposal. The Bavarian Minister Wilhelm Hoegner supported the refusal and they were able to win over the occupation forces and the ministerial advisory committee. The Kehlsteinhaus is the only surviving witness to the Nazi era at Obersalzberg and is now a popular mountaintop restaurant with breathtaking panoramic views. (USHHM and Tobi85)